Favorite Recorder Tunes

Beautiful Airs and Ballads of the British Isles

Marcia Diehl

The Rottenburgh Baroque recorder model 4204 of boxwood on our cover is courtesy of Moeck Musikinstrumente + Verlag GmbH, Celle - Germany.

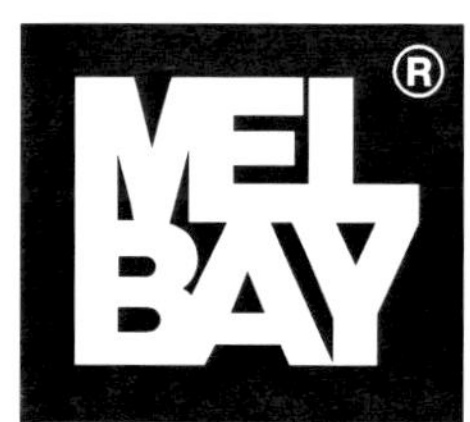

WWW. MELBAY.COM

Preface

The 41 tunes in this collection were arranged for the soprano and tenor recorders. They fit within the comfortable range of both instruments.

A collection of *Beautiful Airs and Ballads of the British Isles* would not be complete without tunes by Turlough O'Carolan, the prolific Irish composer and Celtic harpist of the 1700s. Classical influences can be heard in his works "Lord Inchiquin" and "Eleanor Plunkett". Accompanied by a caretaker, the blind O'Carolan roamed throughout Ireland, playing for his keep and composing tunes named after his patrons. His vast body of work includes over 200 tunes.

"O Gentle Dove" and "Cuckoo Dear" are examples of the strong tradition of song in Wales.

Another popular traditional tune of northern England and Scotland, "Bonny at Morn", was later arranged for soprano voice and harp by the classical 20th century British composer, Benjamin Britten.

The "Skye Boat Song" was originally written to commemorate the journey of Prince Charles Edward Stuart to the Isle of Skye as he evaded capture after his defeat at the Battle of Culloden. Later the song evolved into a tender lullaby.

The haunting, modal melodies of "The Dark Slender Boy" and "Enchanted Valley" express the melancholic heart and soul of the British Isles.

It is with special, heartfelt joy that I present this compilation for your playing and listening pleasure.

I hope you enjoy it.

Marcia Diehl

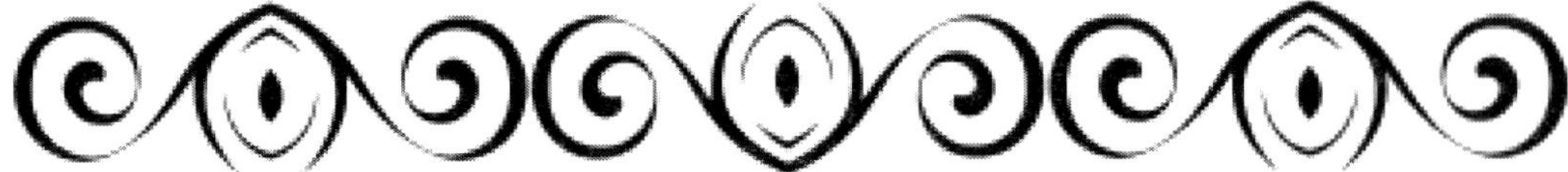

Index

Lord Inchiquin

Turlough O'Carolan

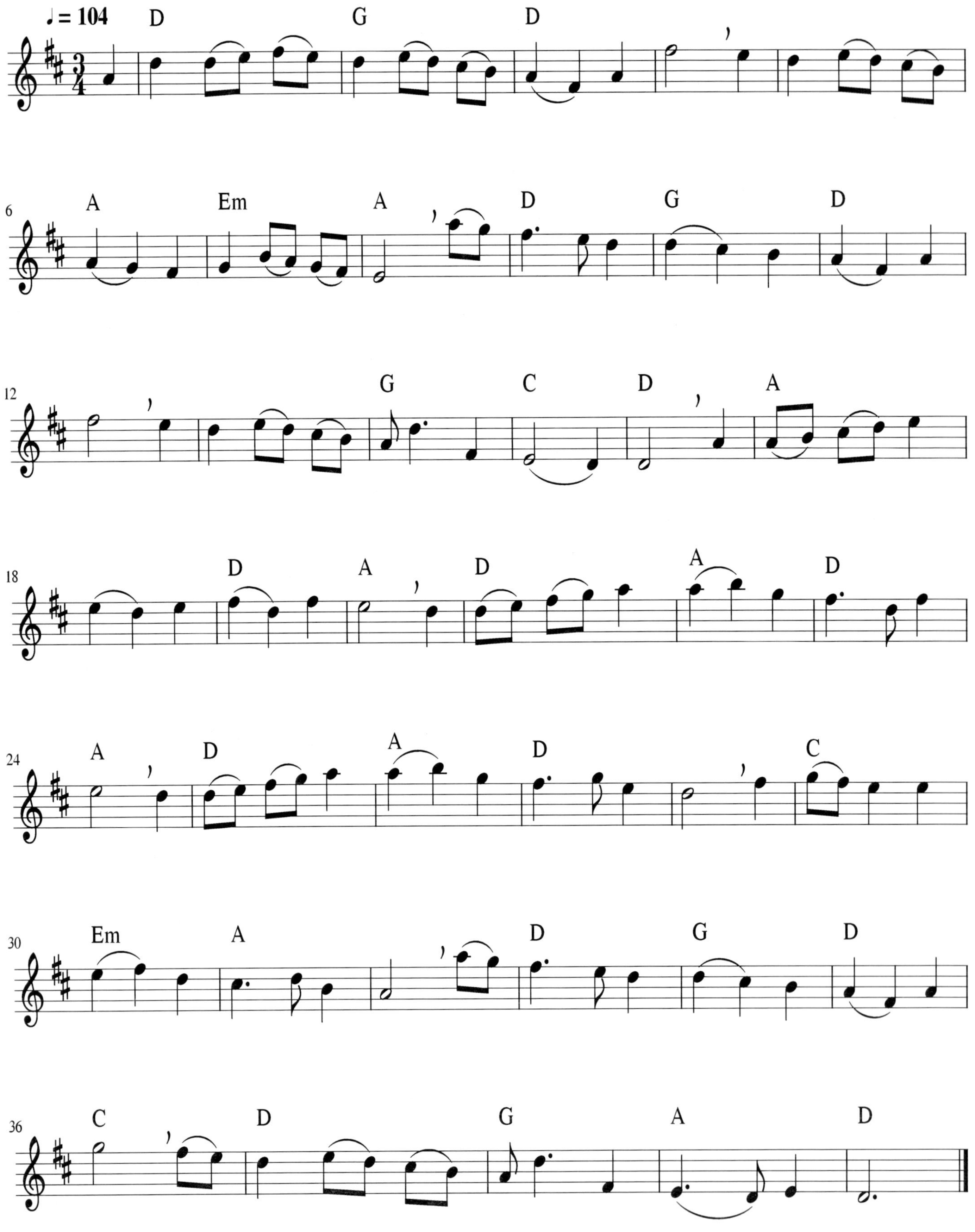

Planxty Irwin

Turlough O'Carolan

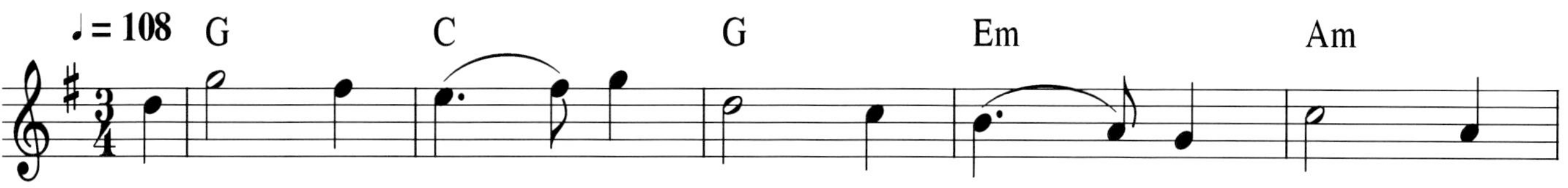

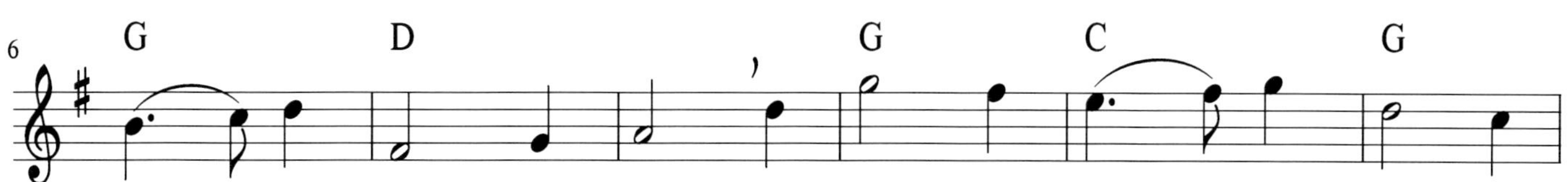

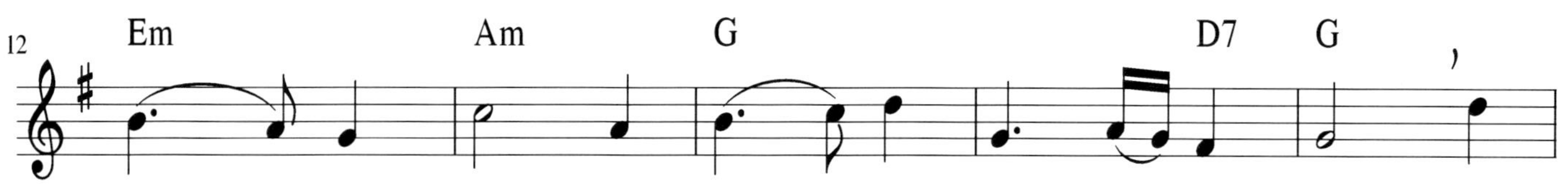

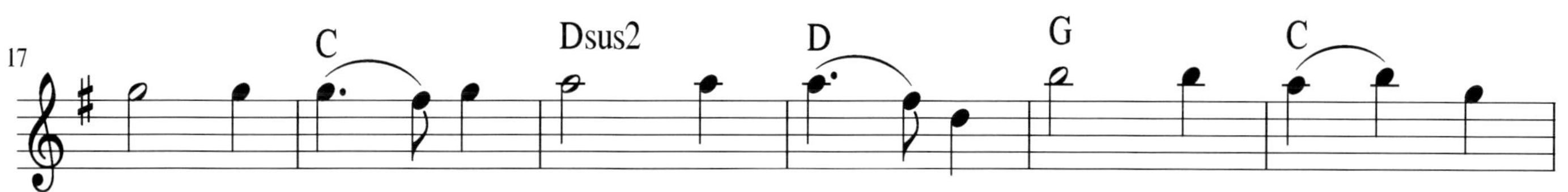

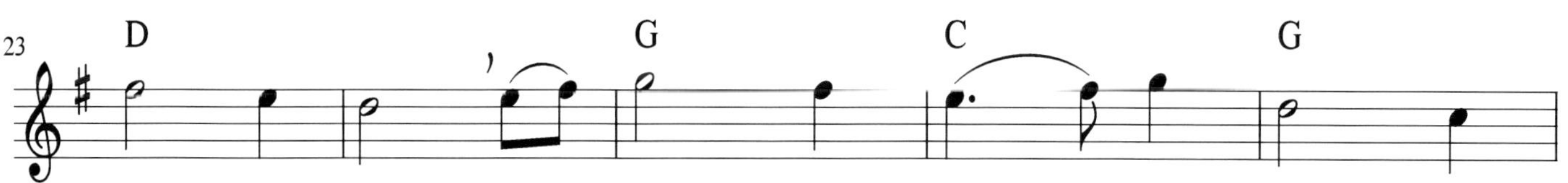

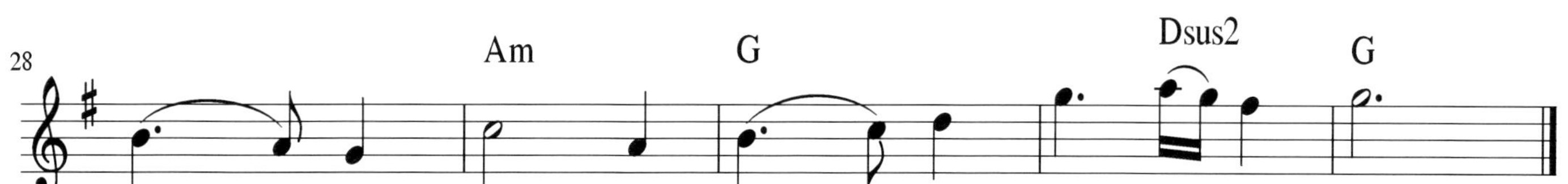

Eleanor Plunkett

for Marion

Turlough O'Carolan

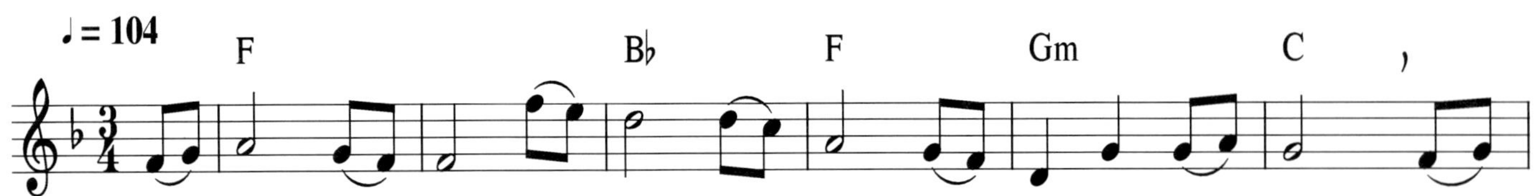

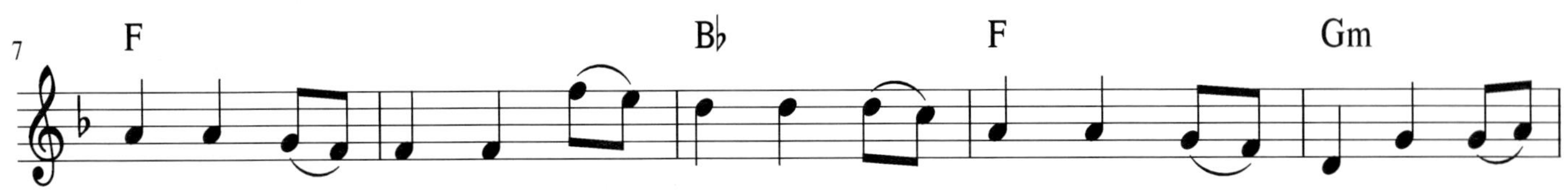

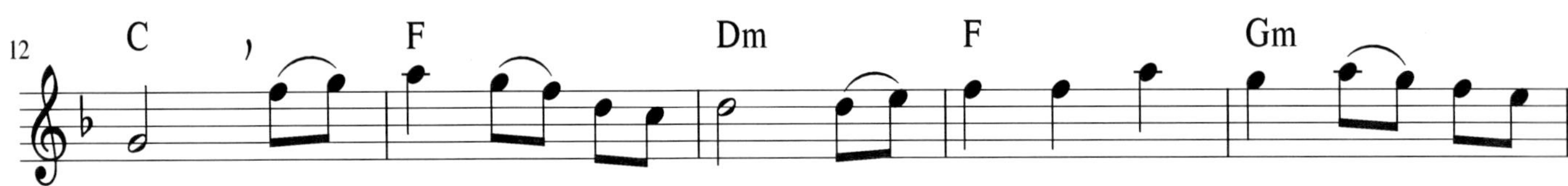

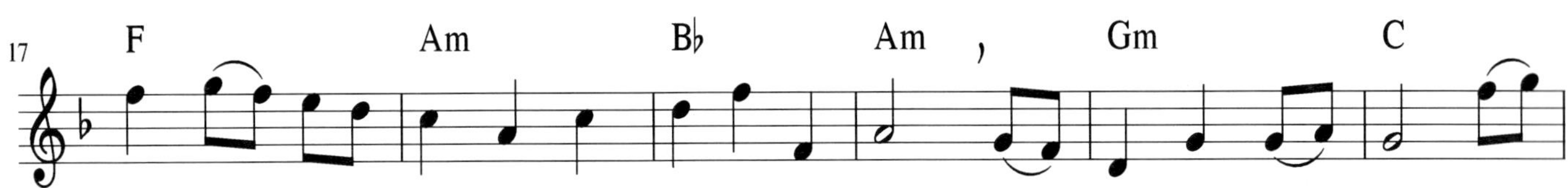

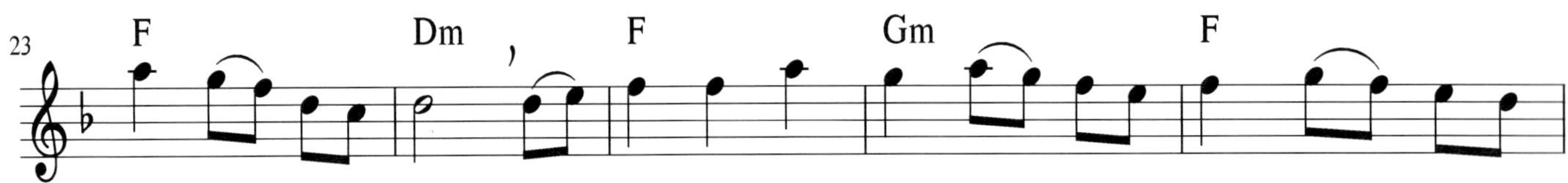

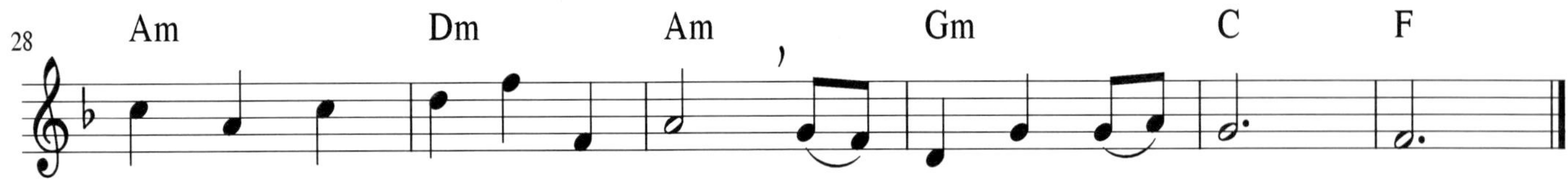

Sheebeg and Sheemor

Turlough O'Carolan

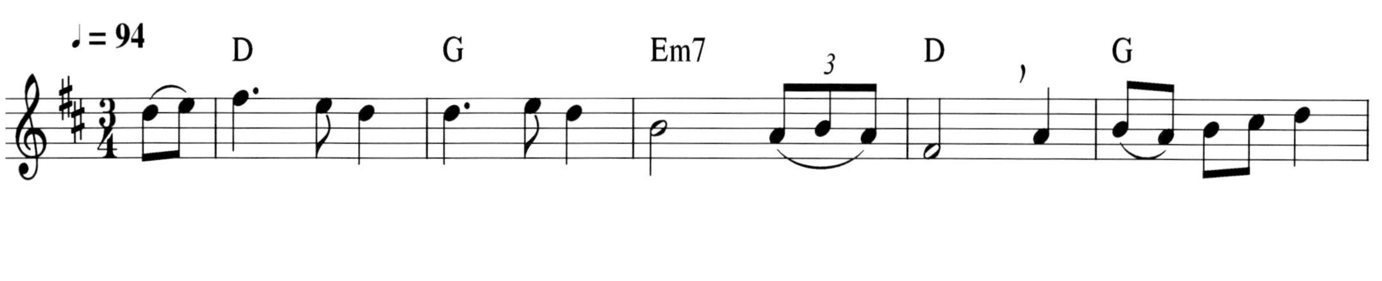

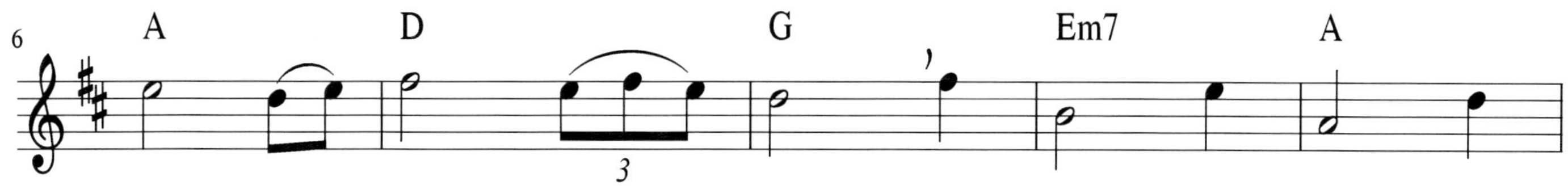

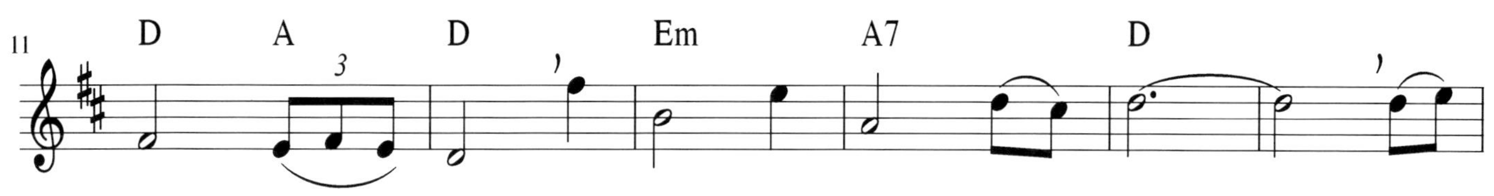

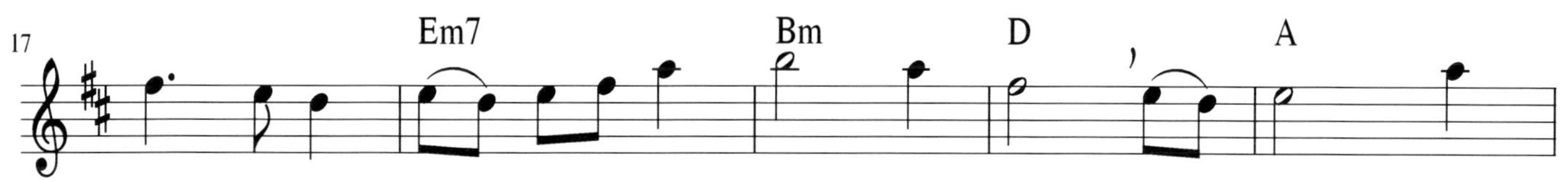

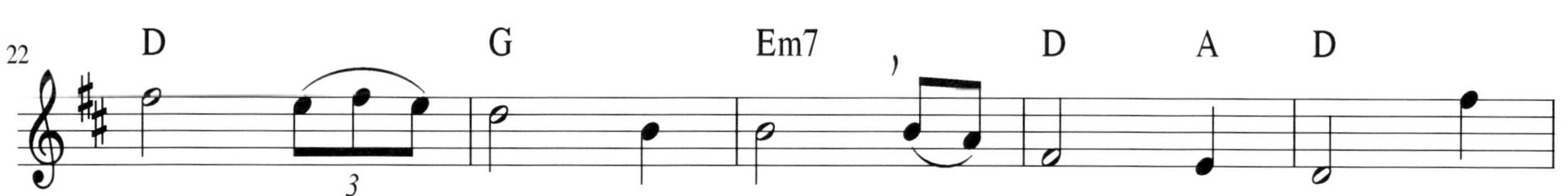

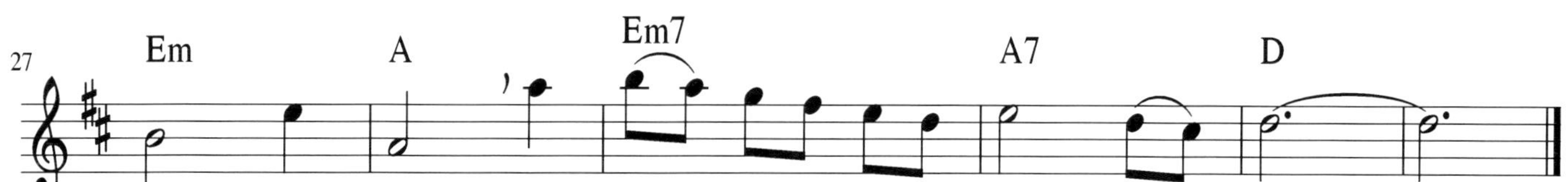

Fanny Power

Turlough O'Carolan

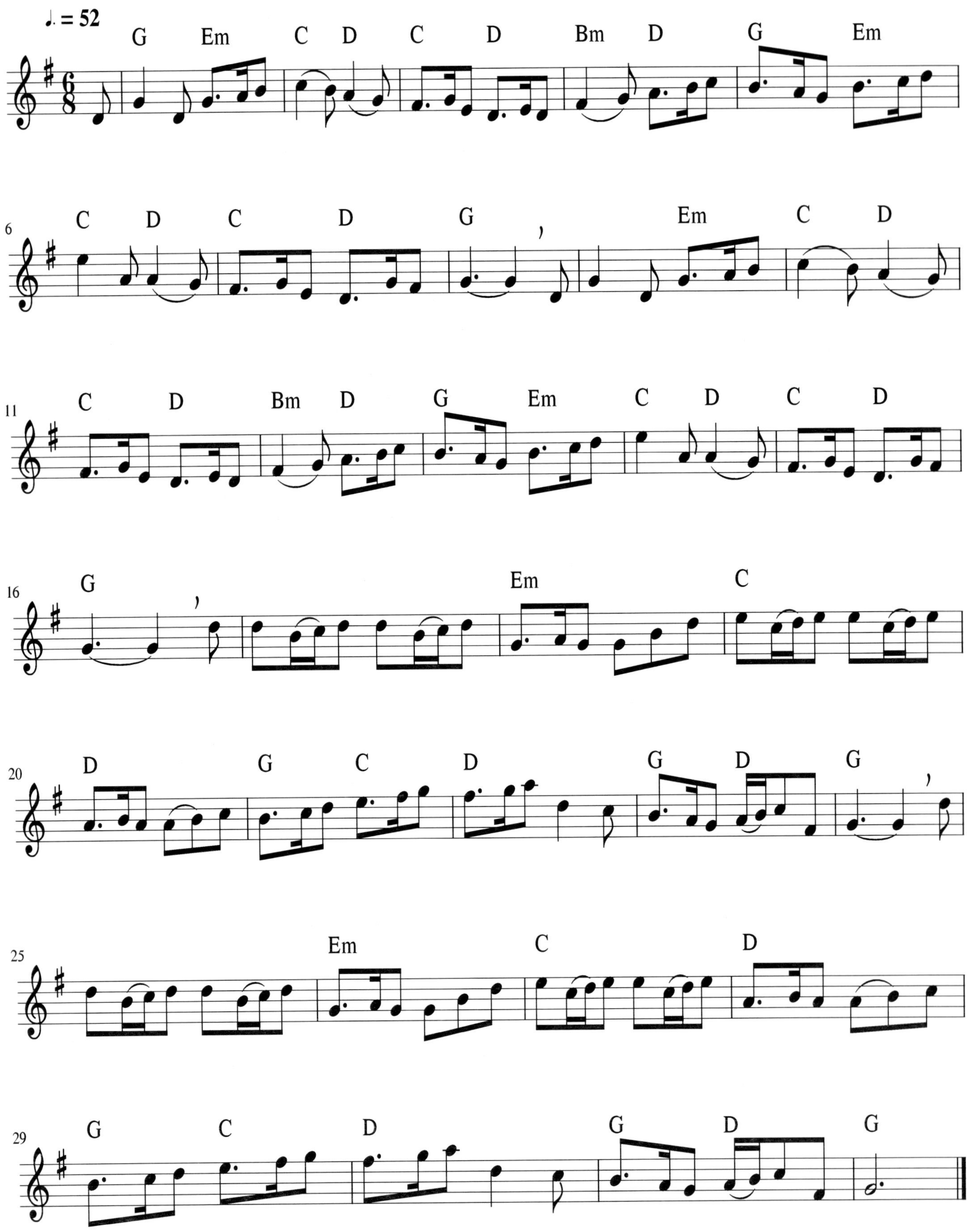

Dear Aileen, I'm Going to Leave You

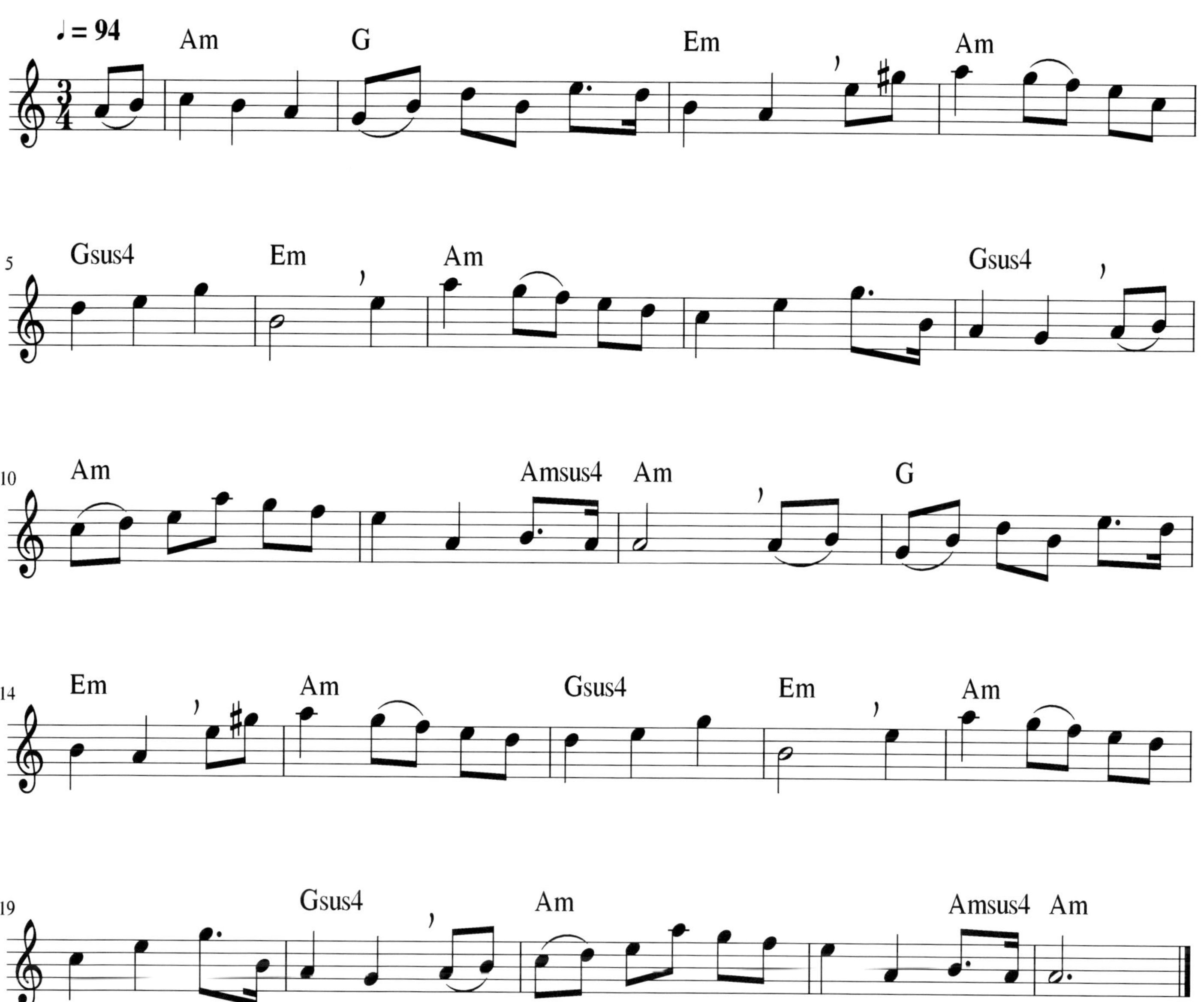

Jock O'Hazeldean

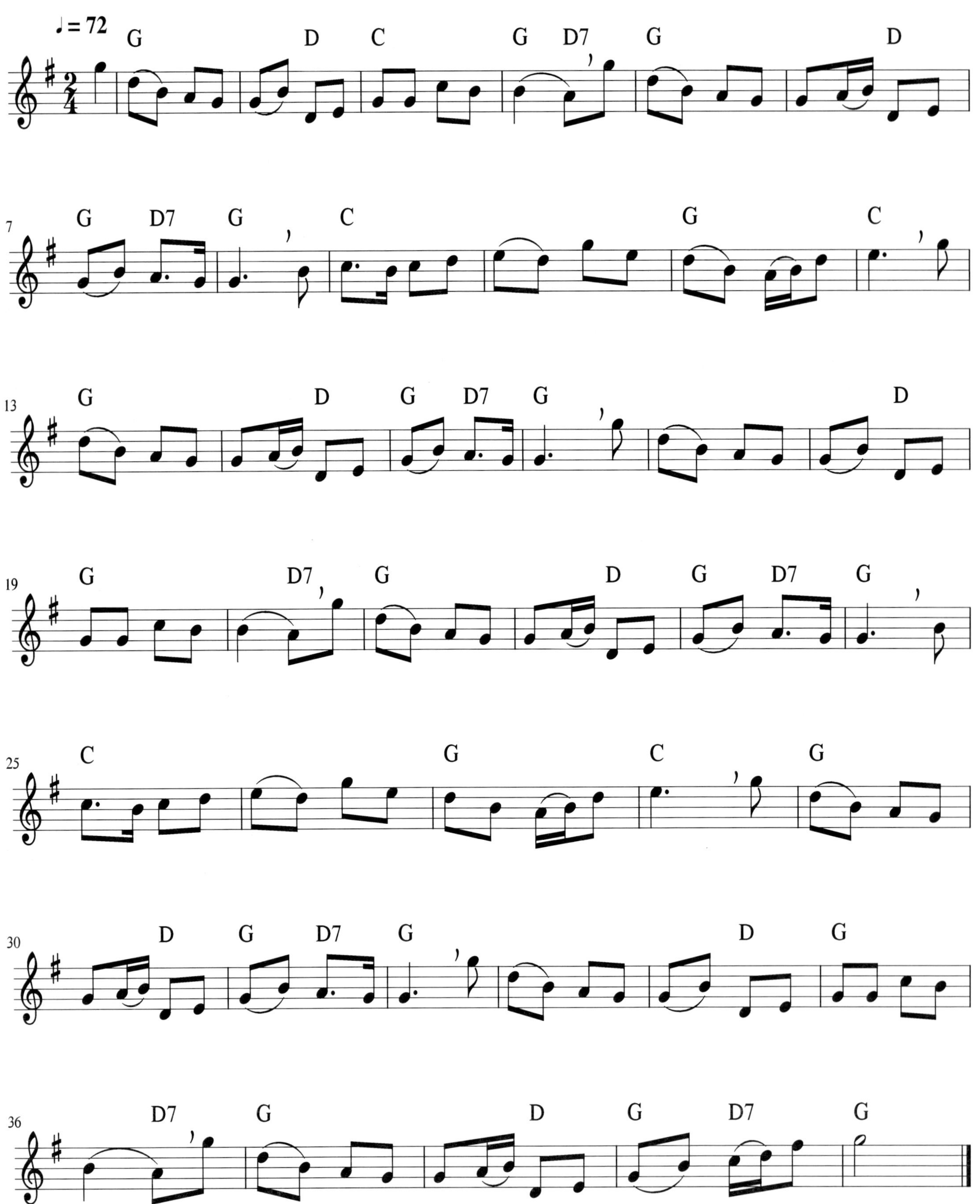

The Dark Slender Boy

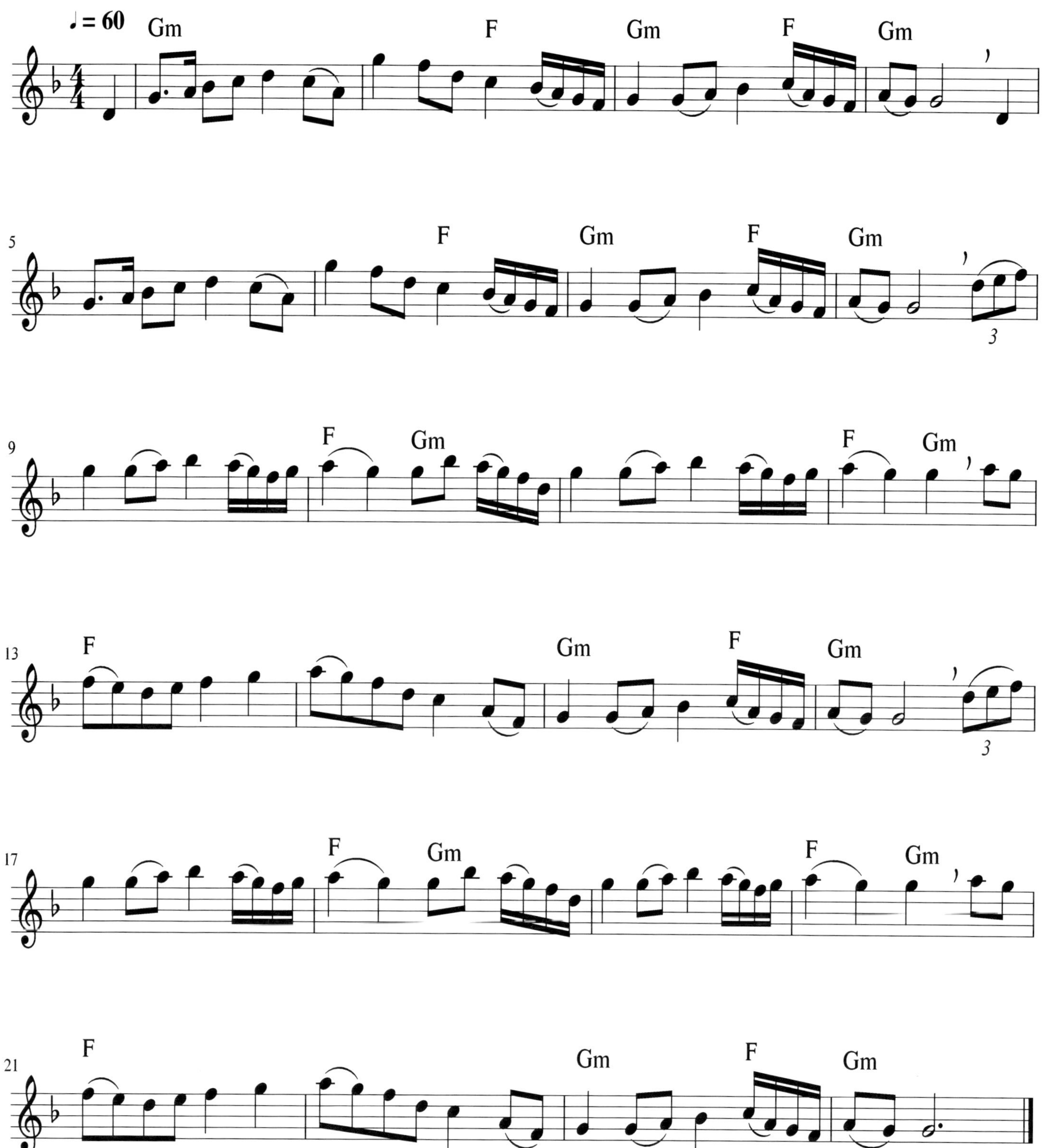

Kitty, My Love

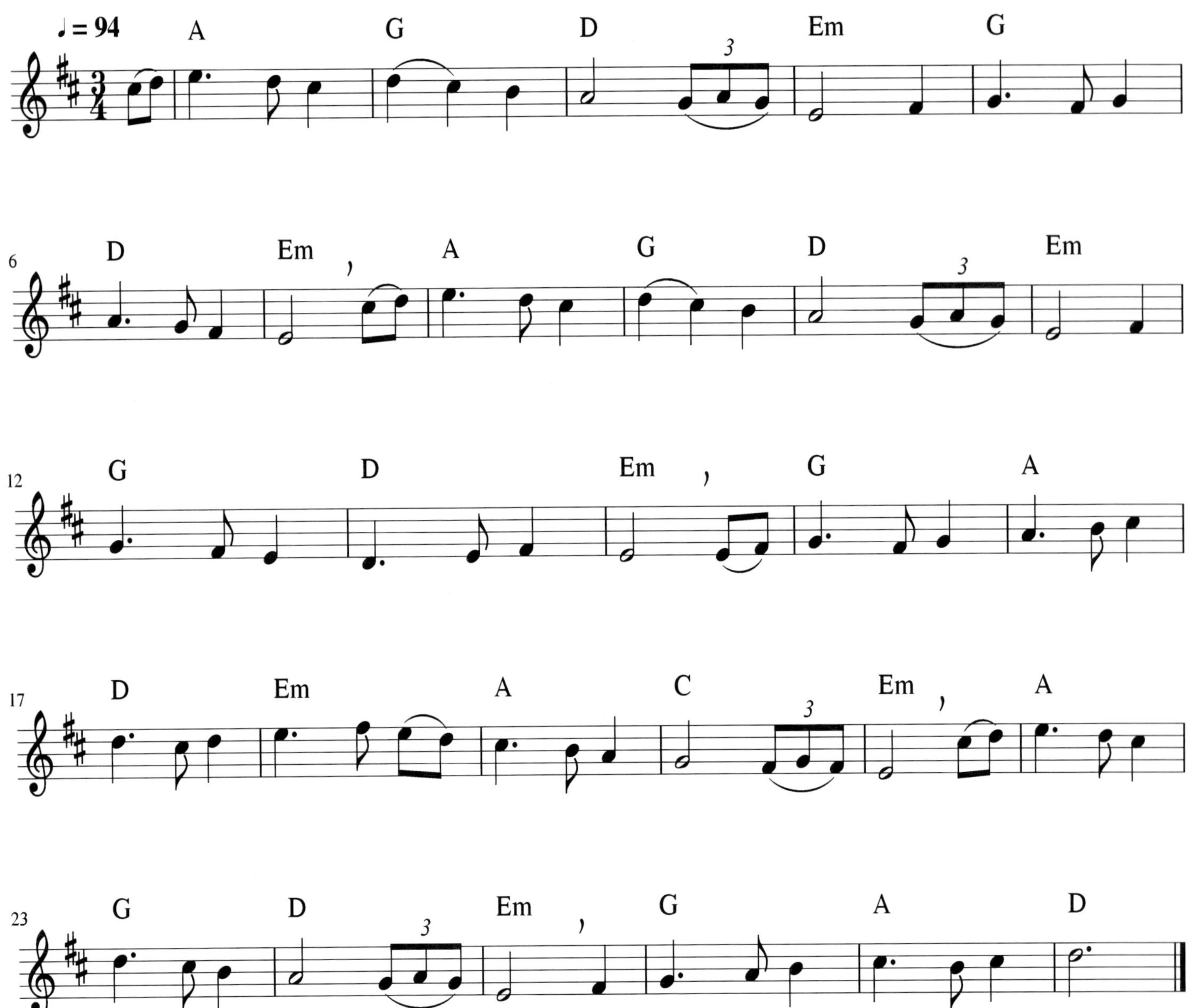

She Moved Through the Fair

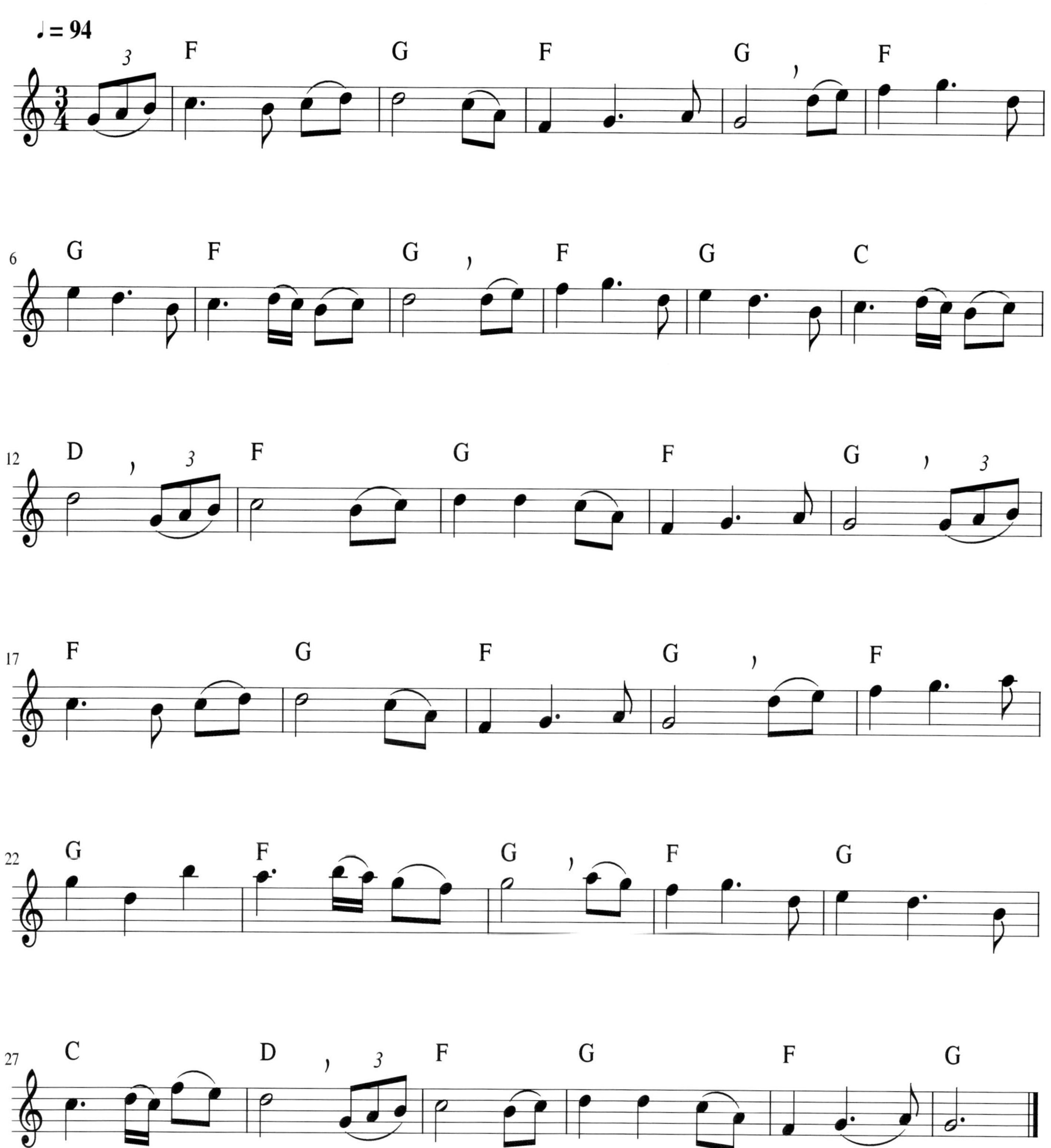

Eamonn a' Chnuic

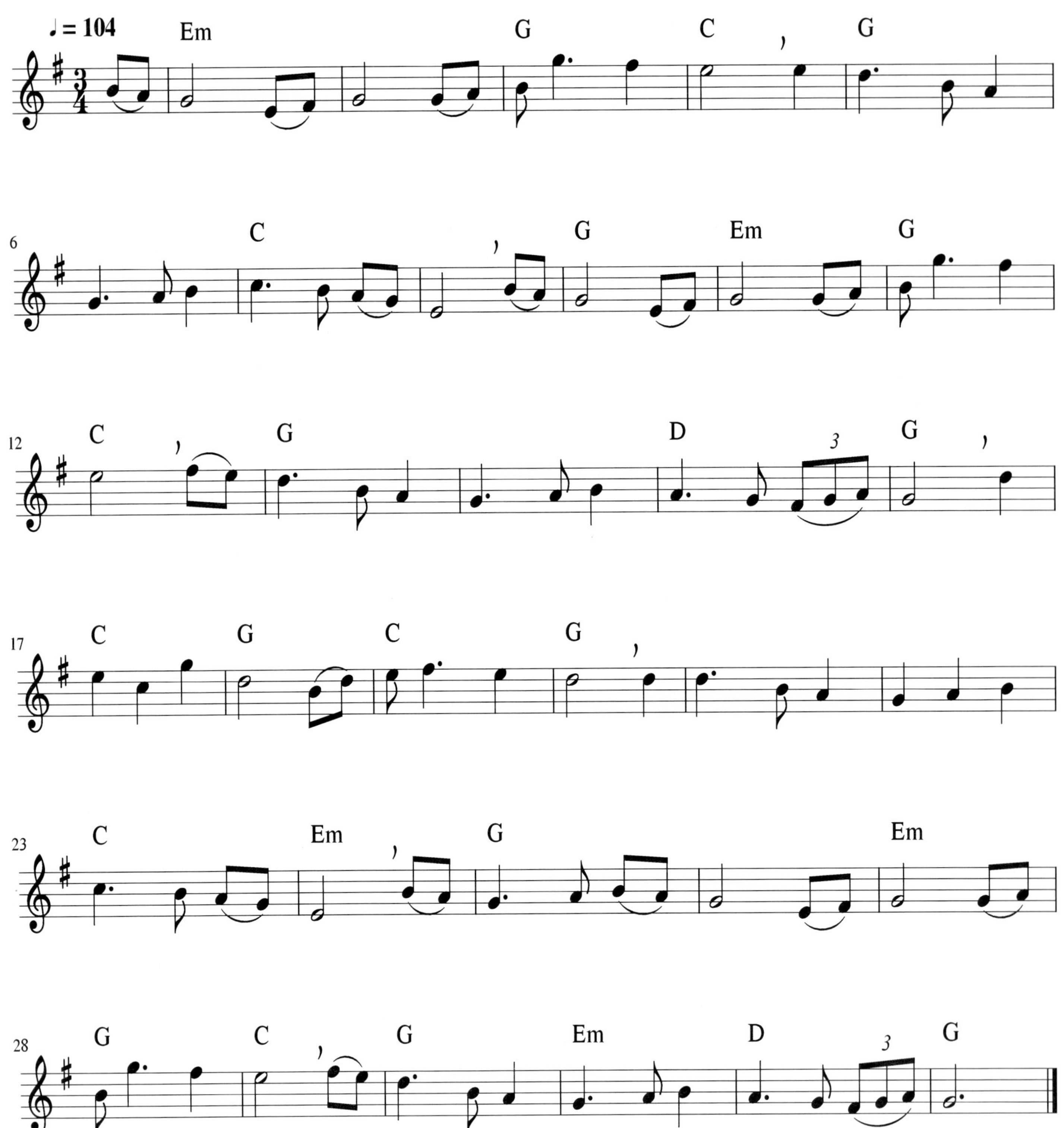

Wild Mountain Thyme

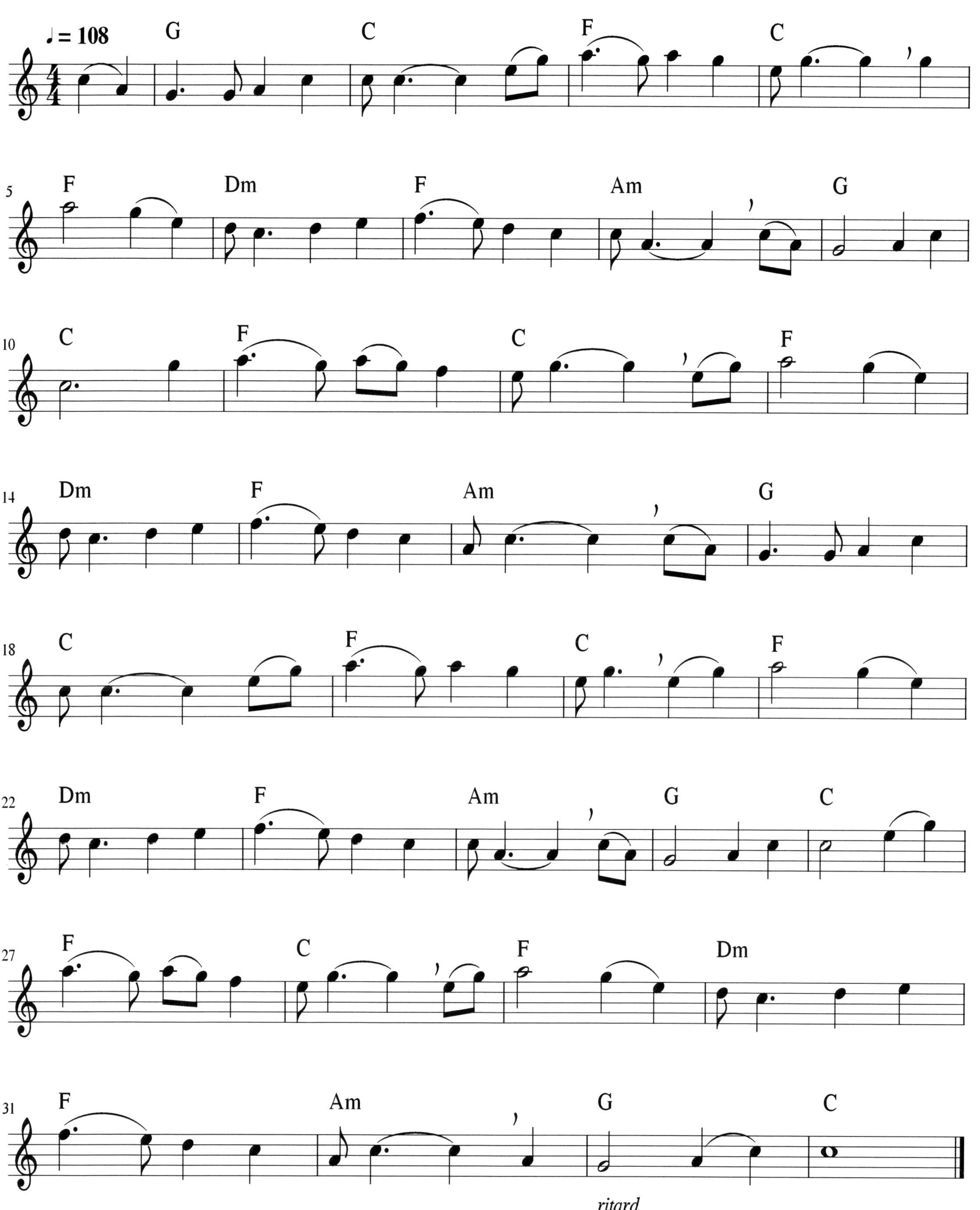

Paistin Fionn

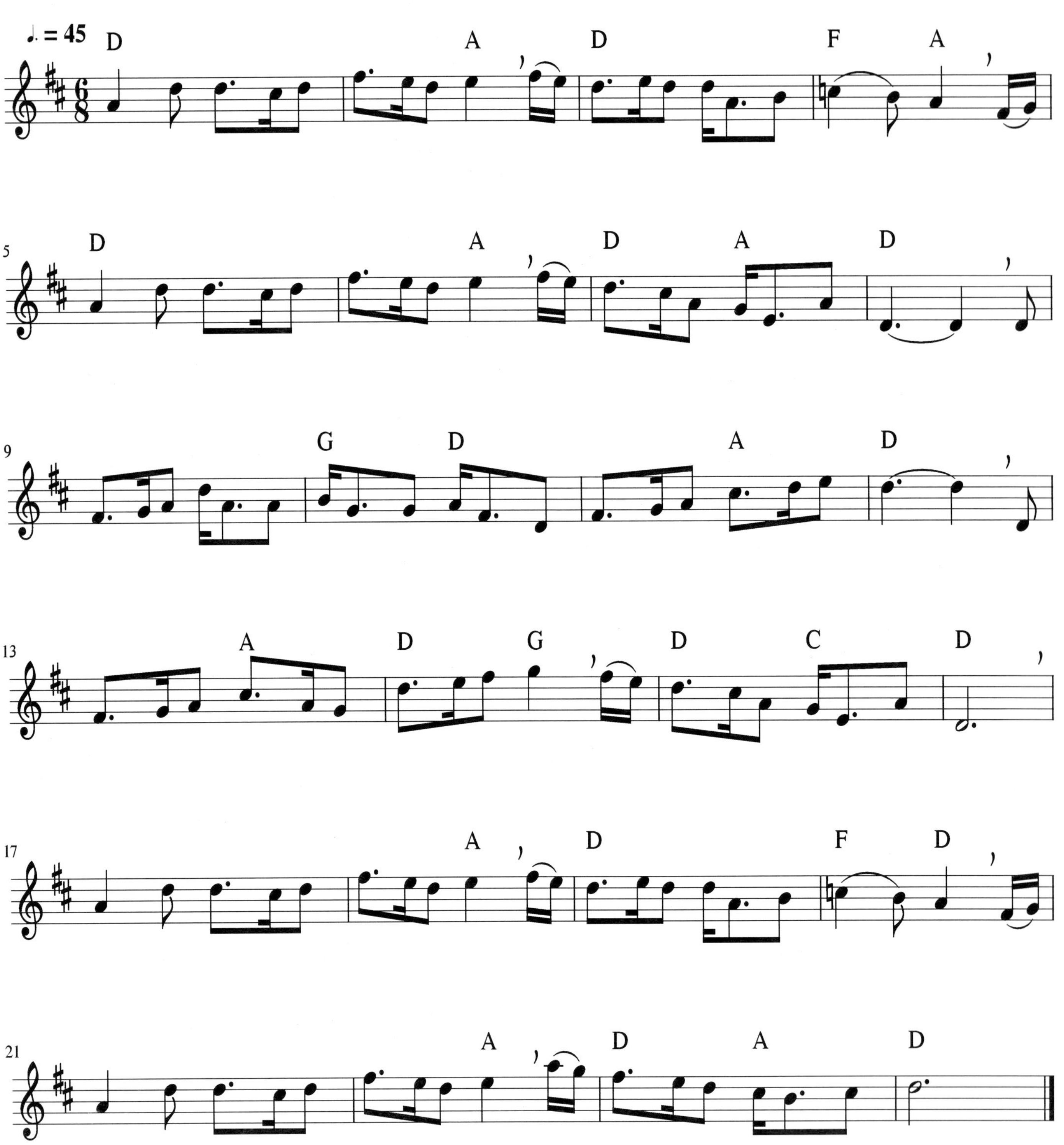

General Monroe's Lament

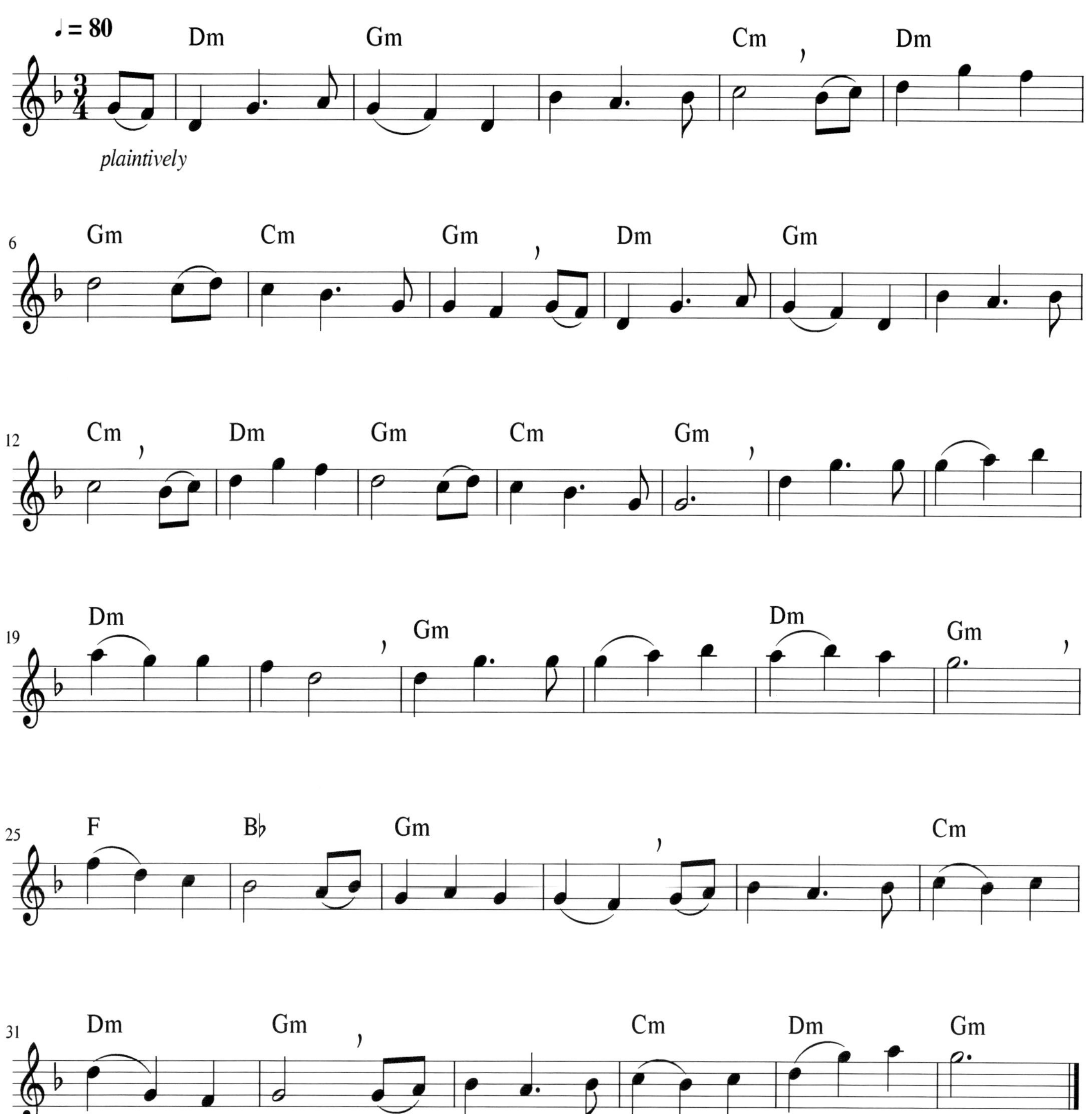

Skye Air

♩ = 82
G
C
G
Em
C
Em
D
G
C
G
Em
C
Em
D
Am
Em
Bm
Em
G
Em
C
Em
Am
D
Am
Em
Bm
Em
G
Em
C
Em
Am

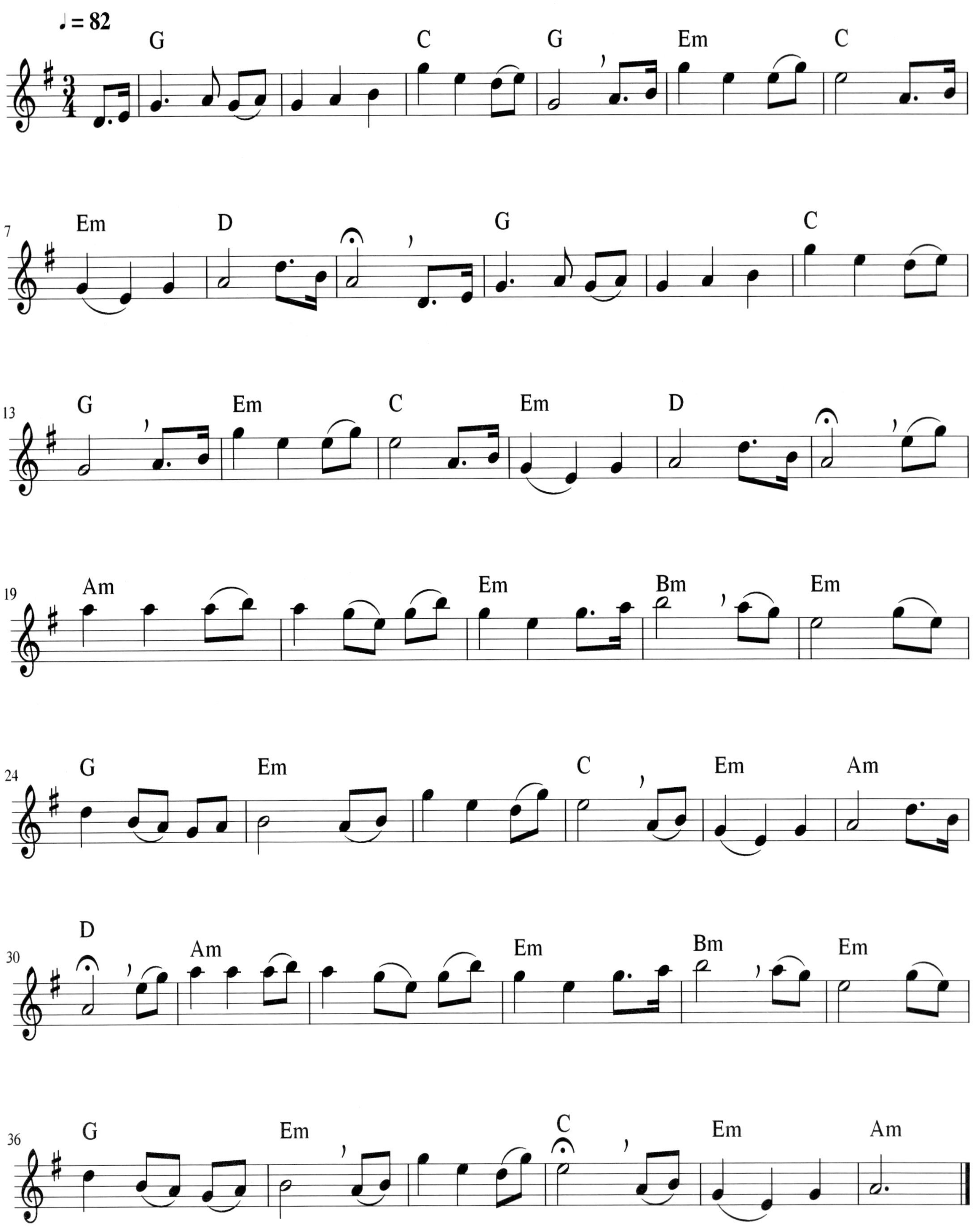

The Pretty Maid Milking Her Cow

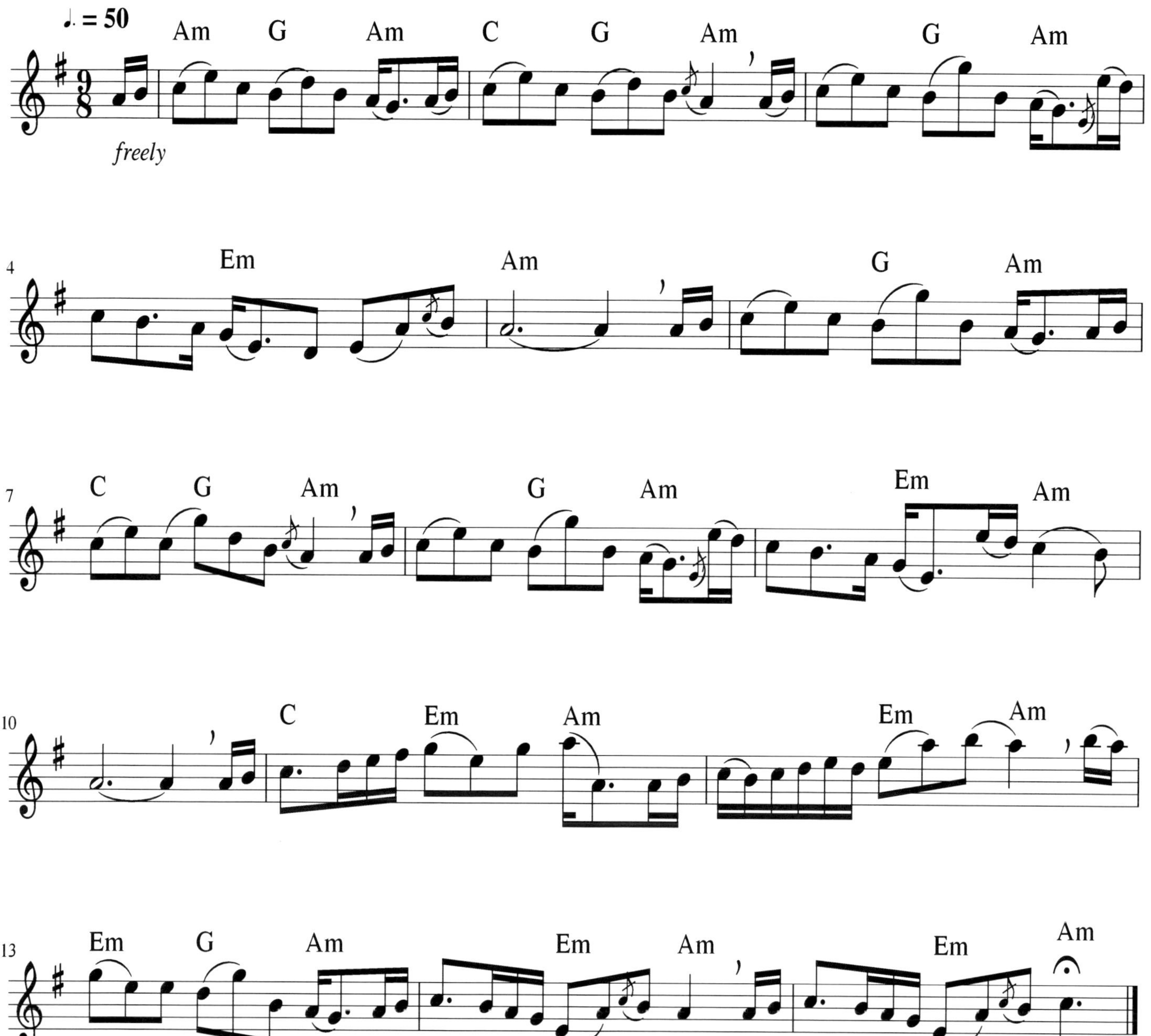

Come by the Hills

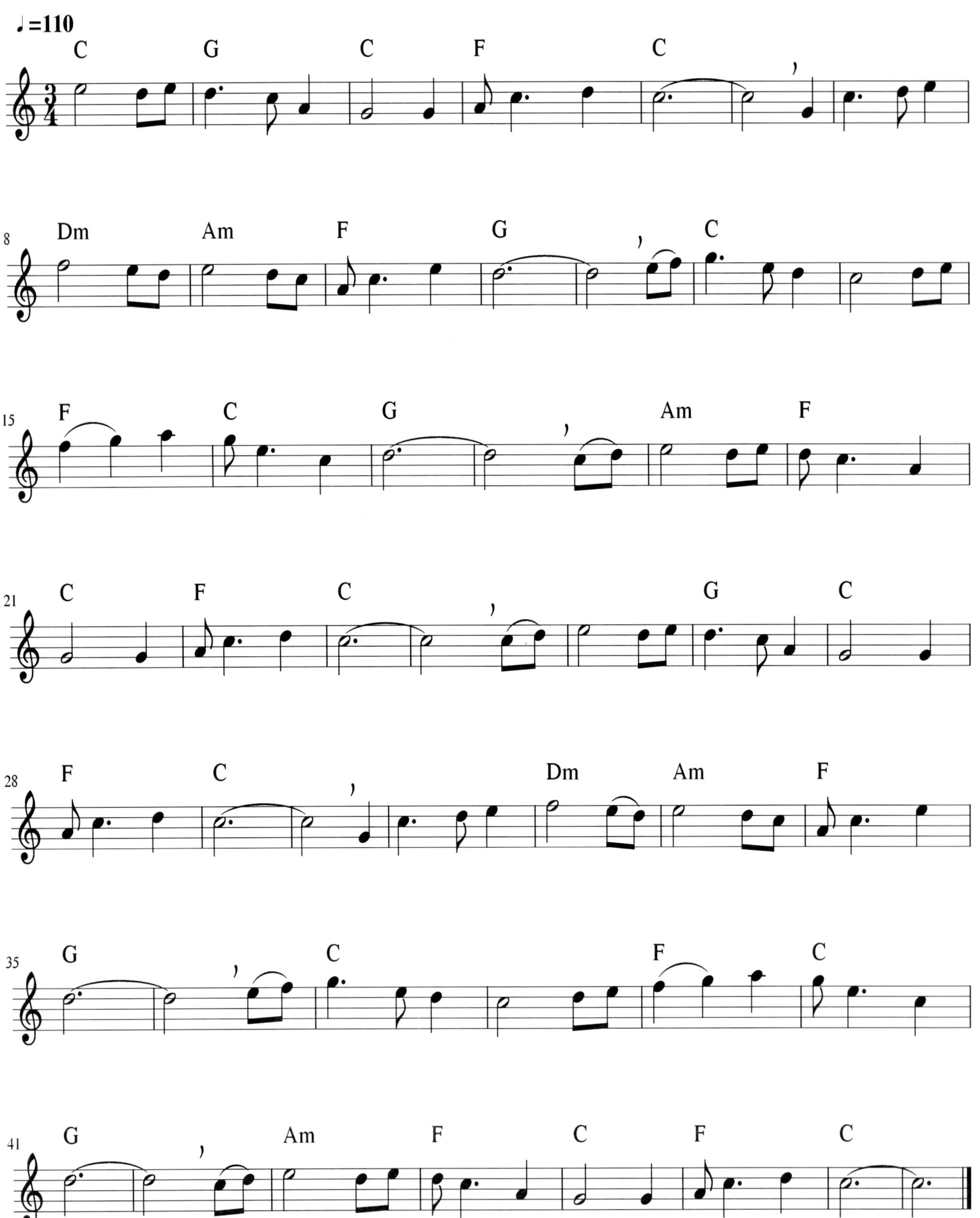

Down by the Sally Gardens

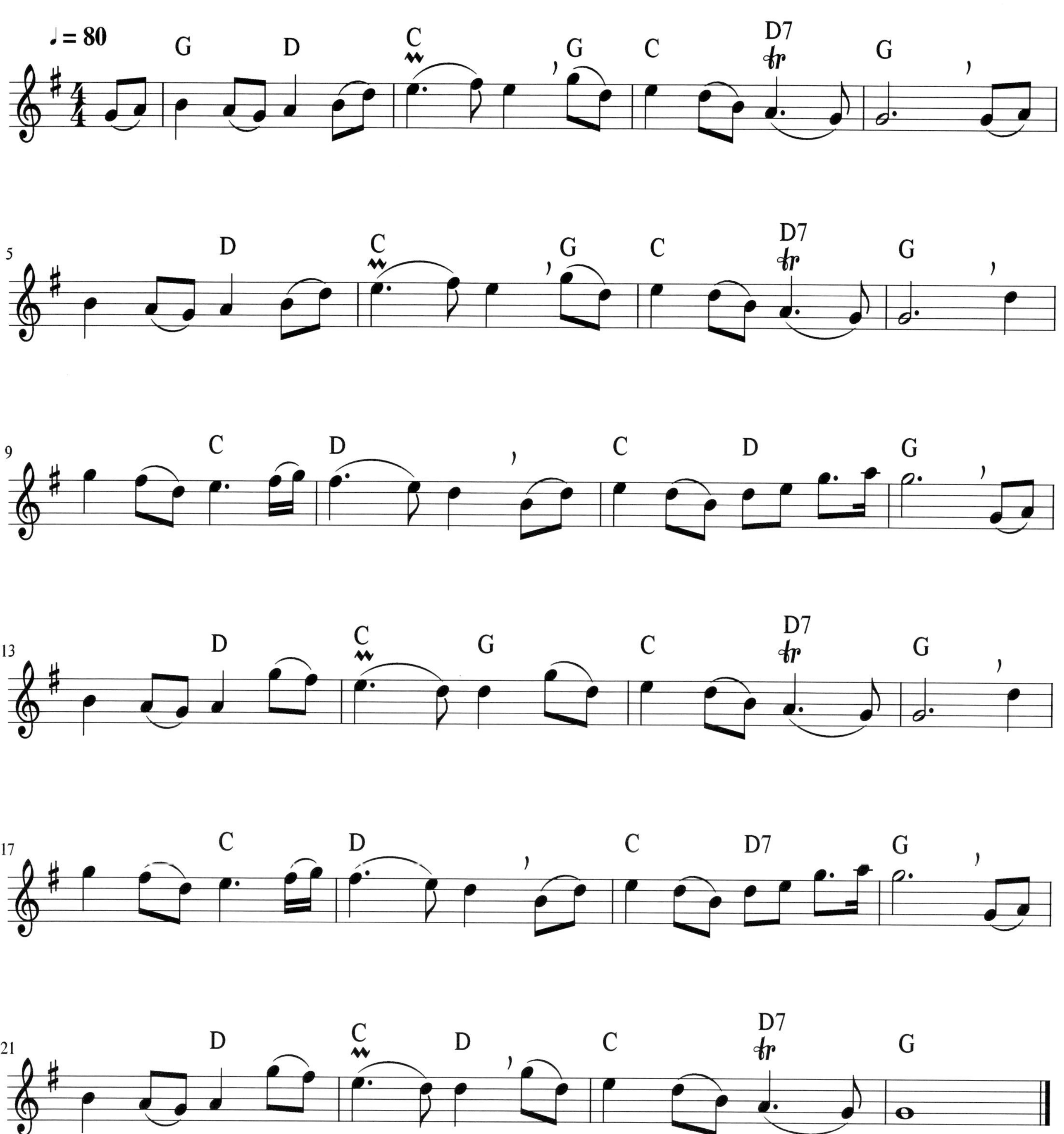

I'm Asleep, Don't Awaken Me

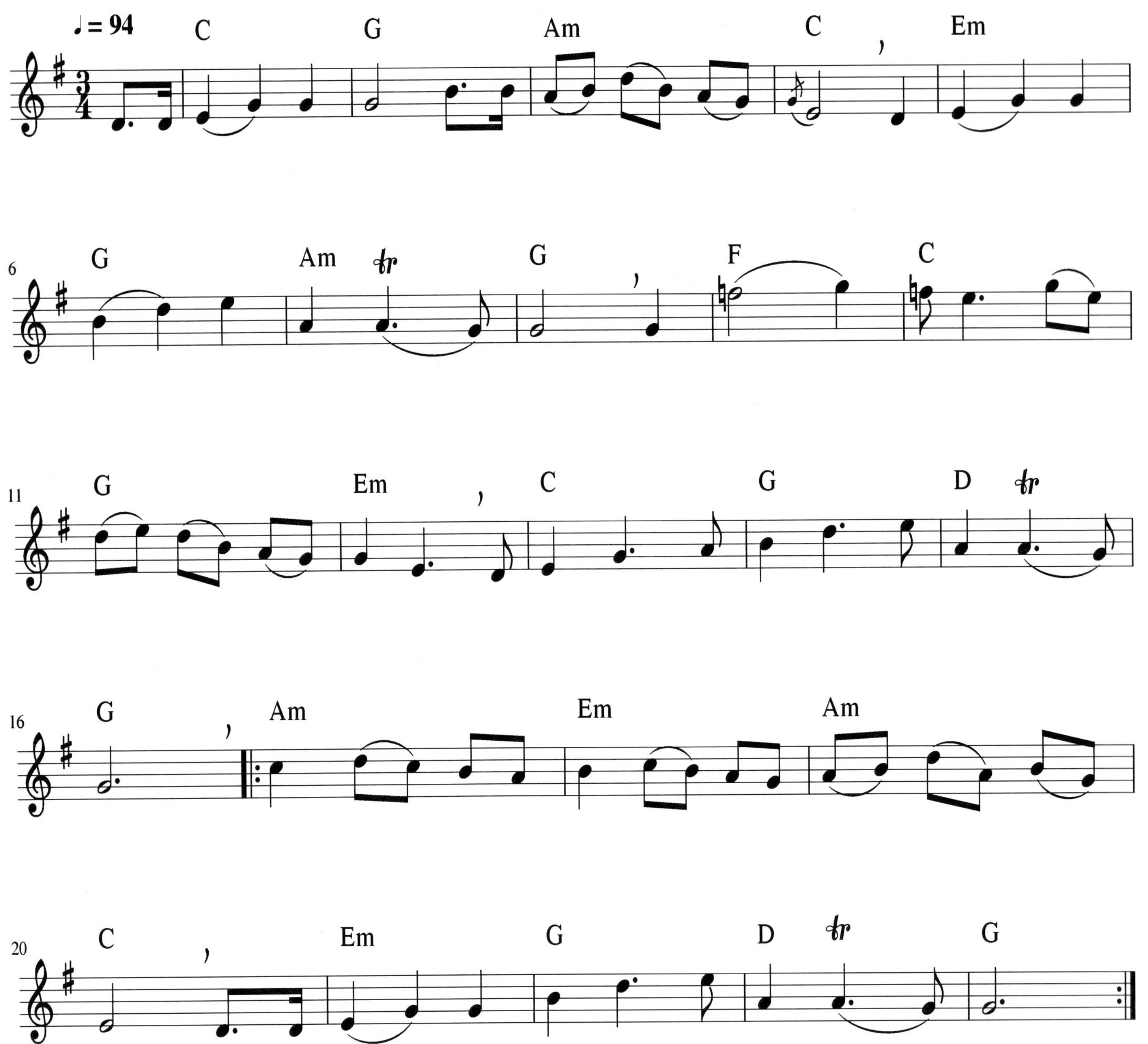

Cuckoo Dear

♩ = 94
Em
Am
Em
G
Em
5
Am
Em
G
Em
9
D
C
B
Em
D
Em
B
13
Em
Am
Em
G
Em

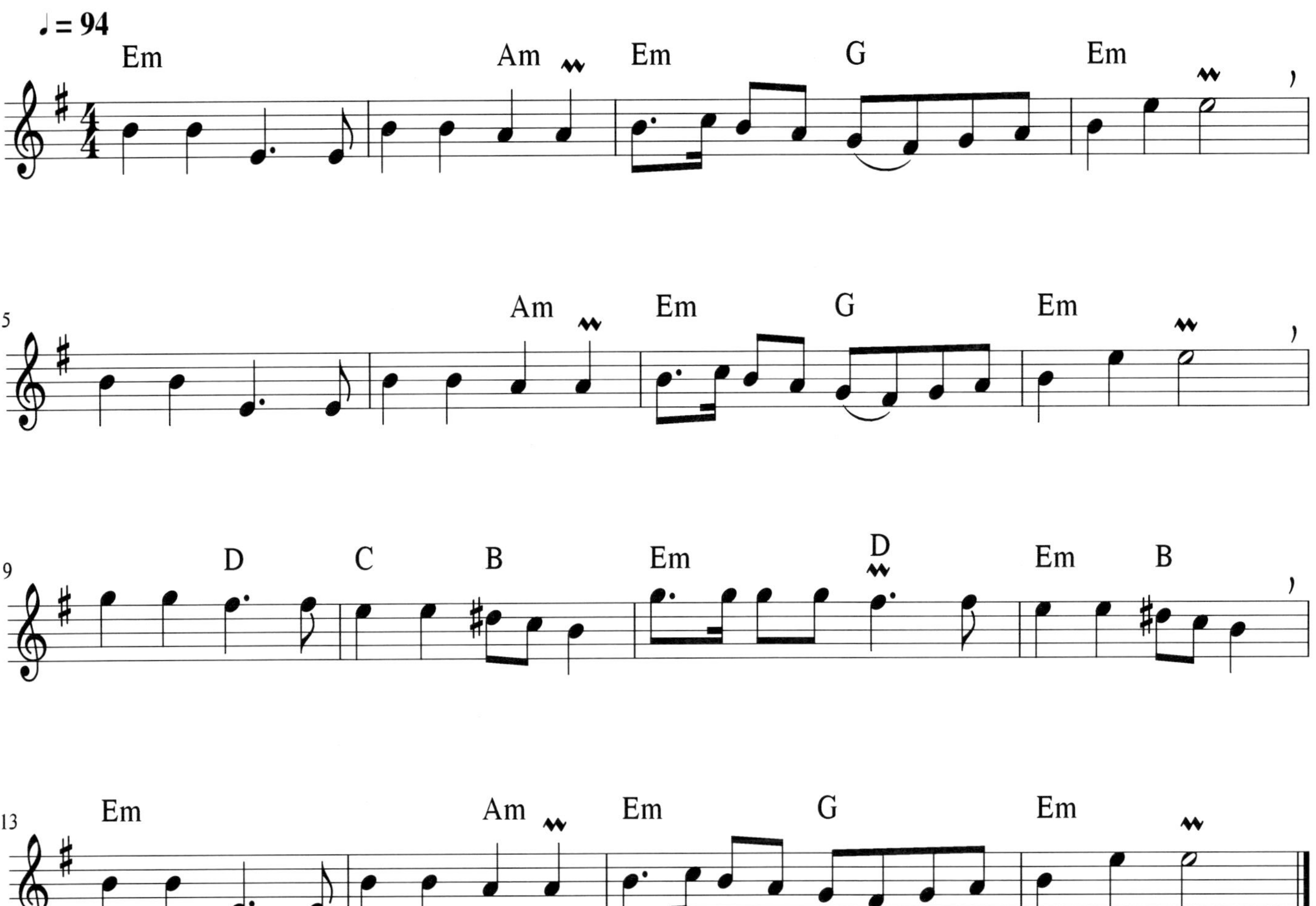

The Dark Island

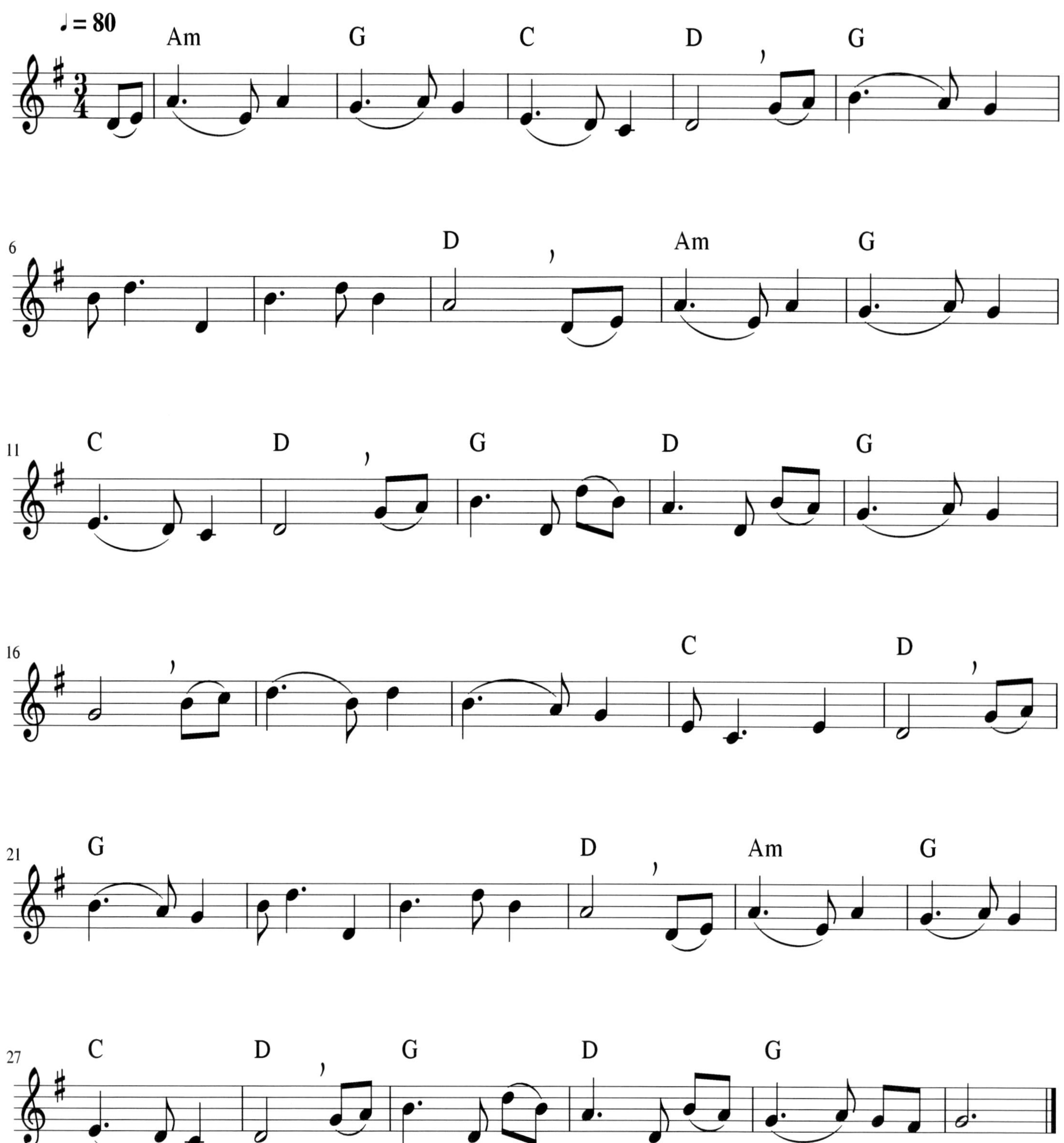

I Wish I Were on Yonder Hill

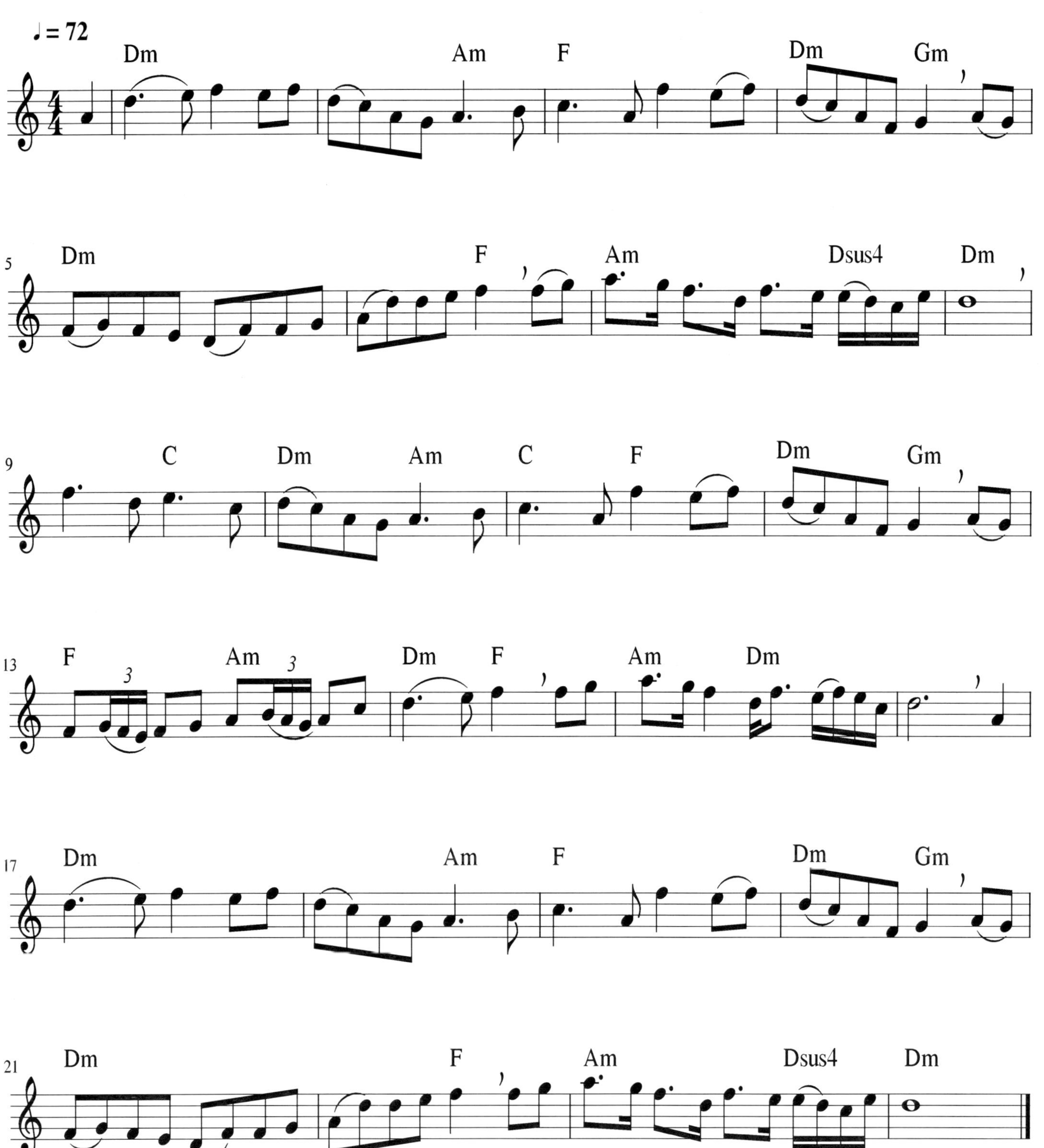

Believe Me if All Those Endearing Charms

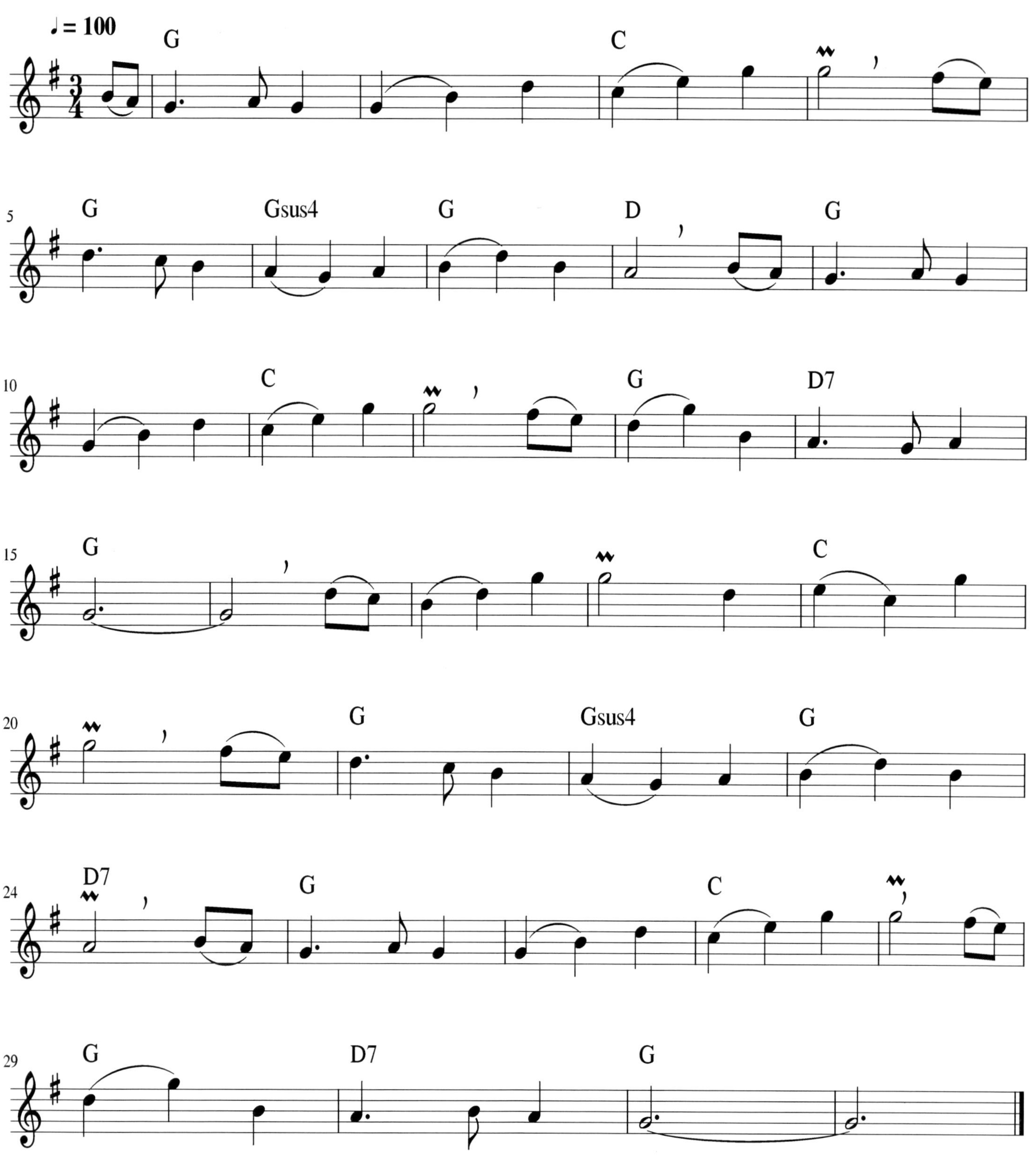

Street Ballad

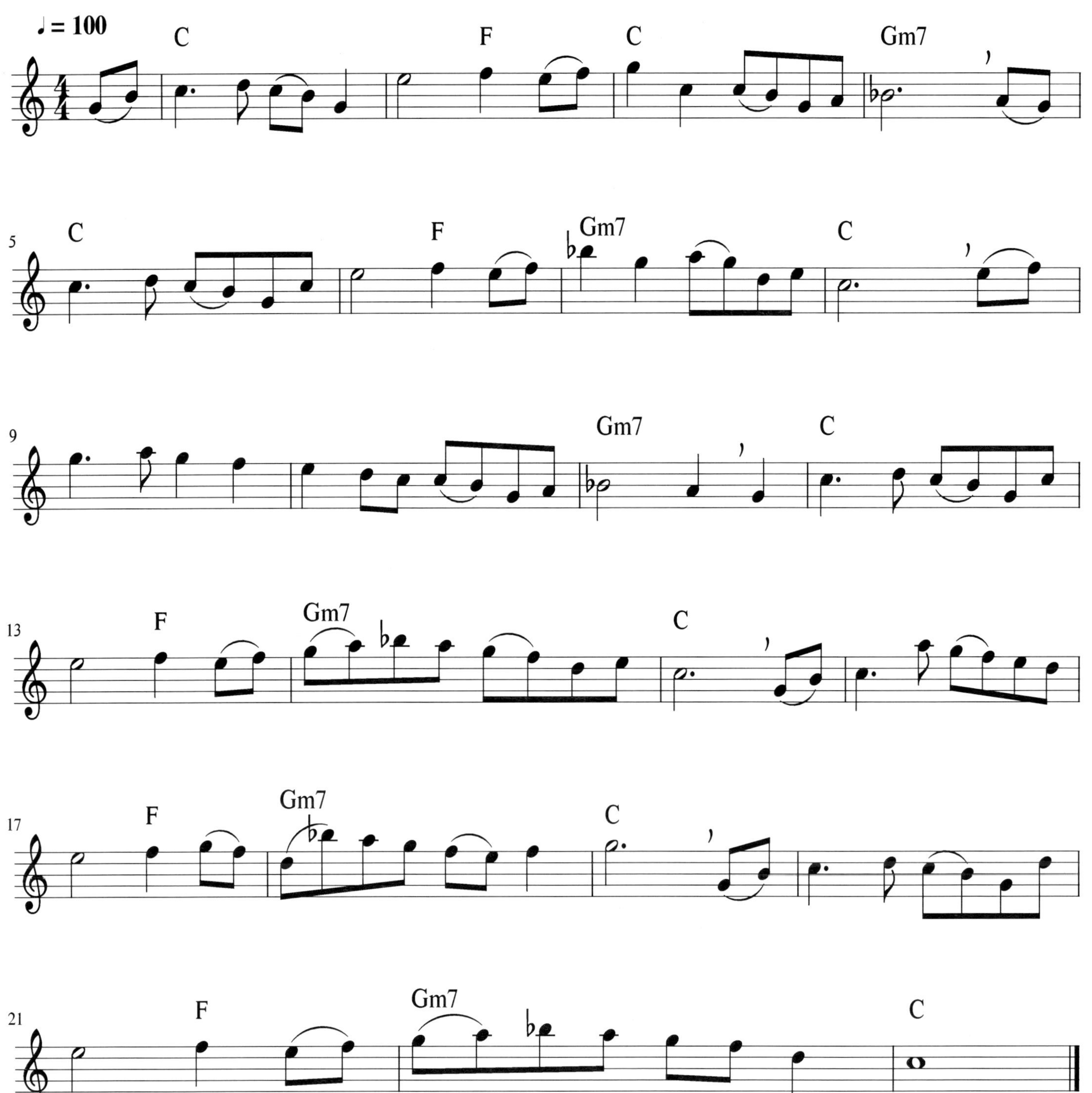

The Marsh of Rhuddlan

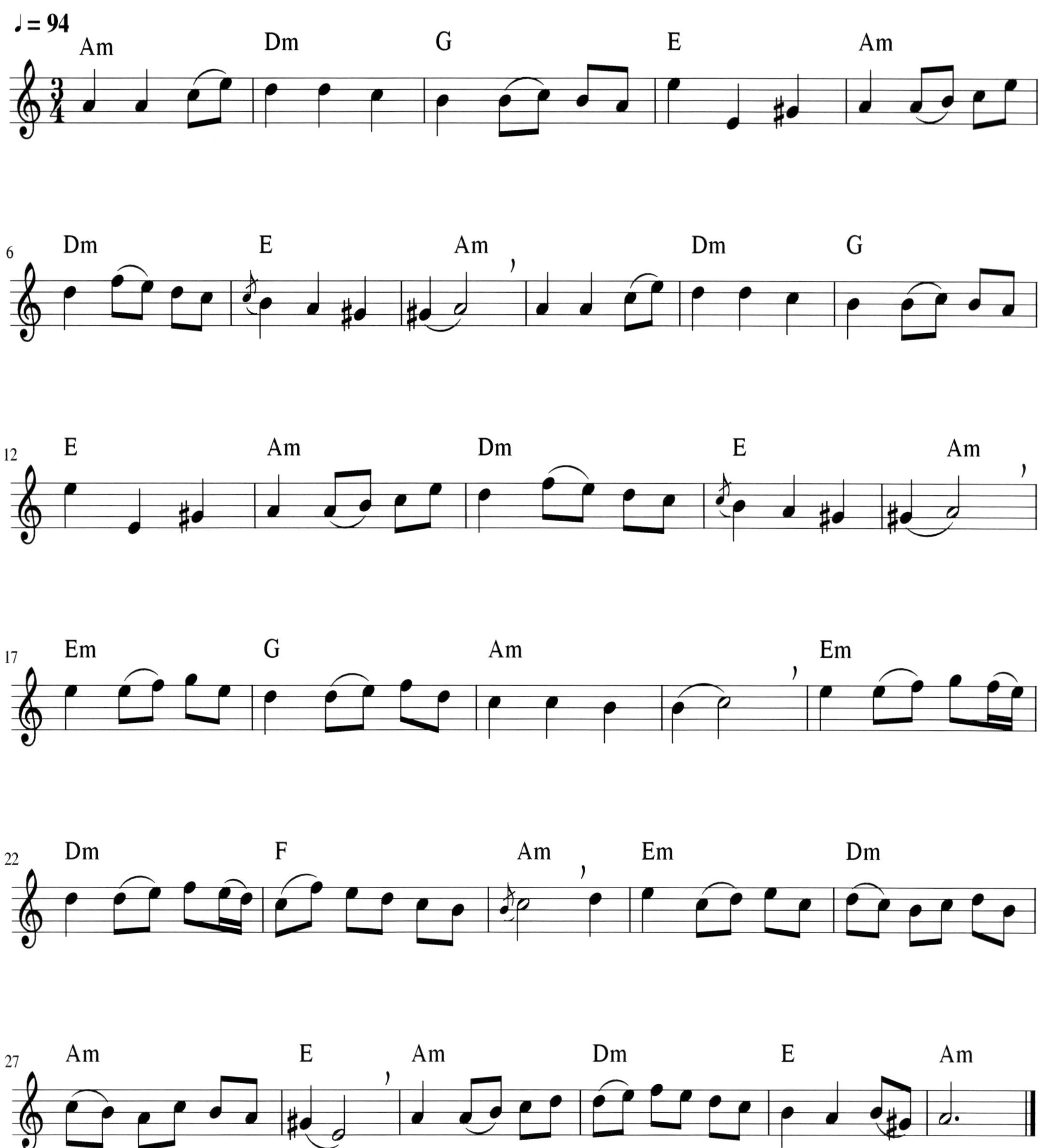

Saint Patrick Was a Gentleman

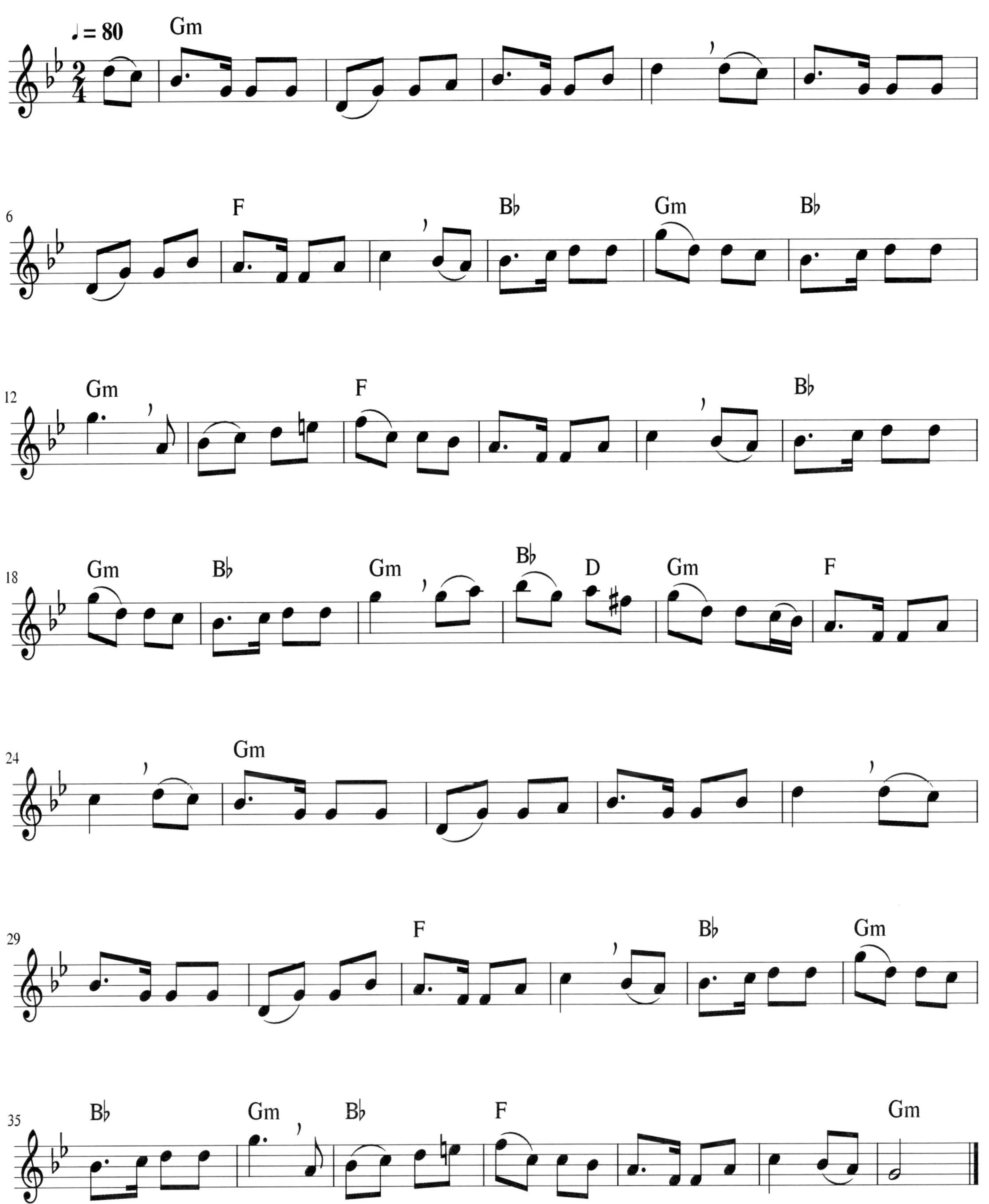

Once I Had a Sweetheart

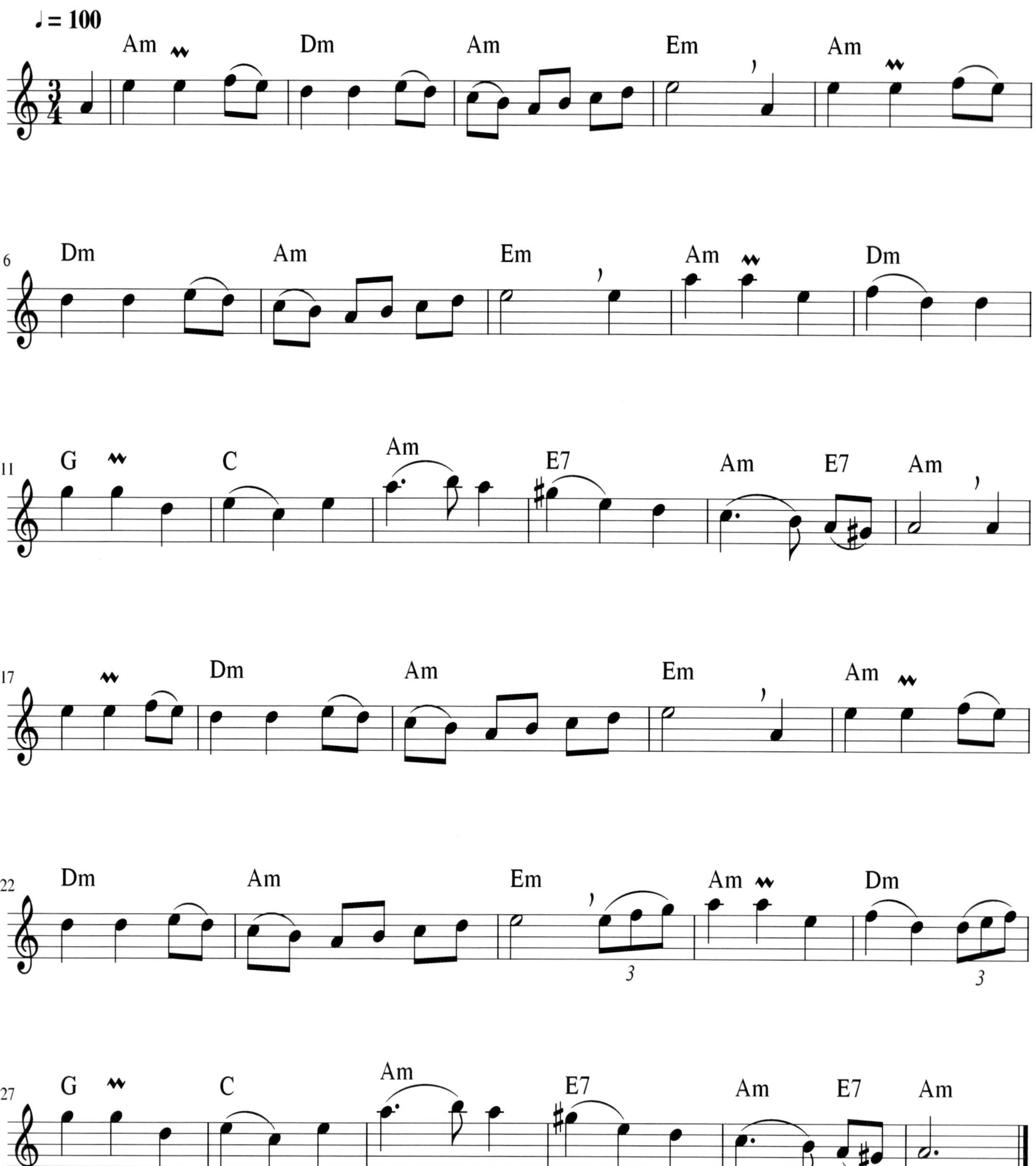

Caitlín Triall

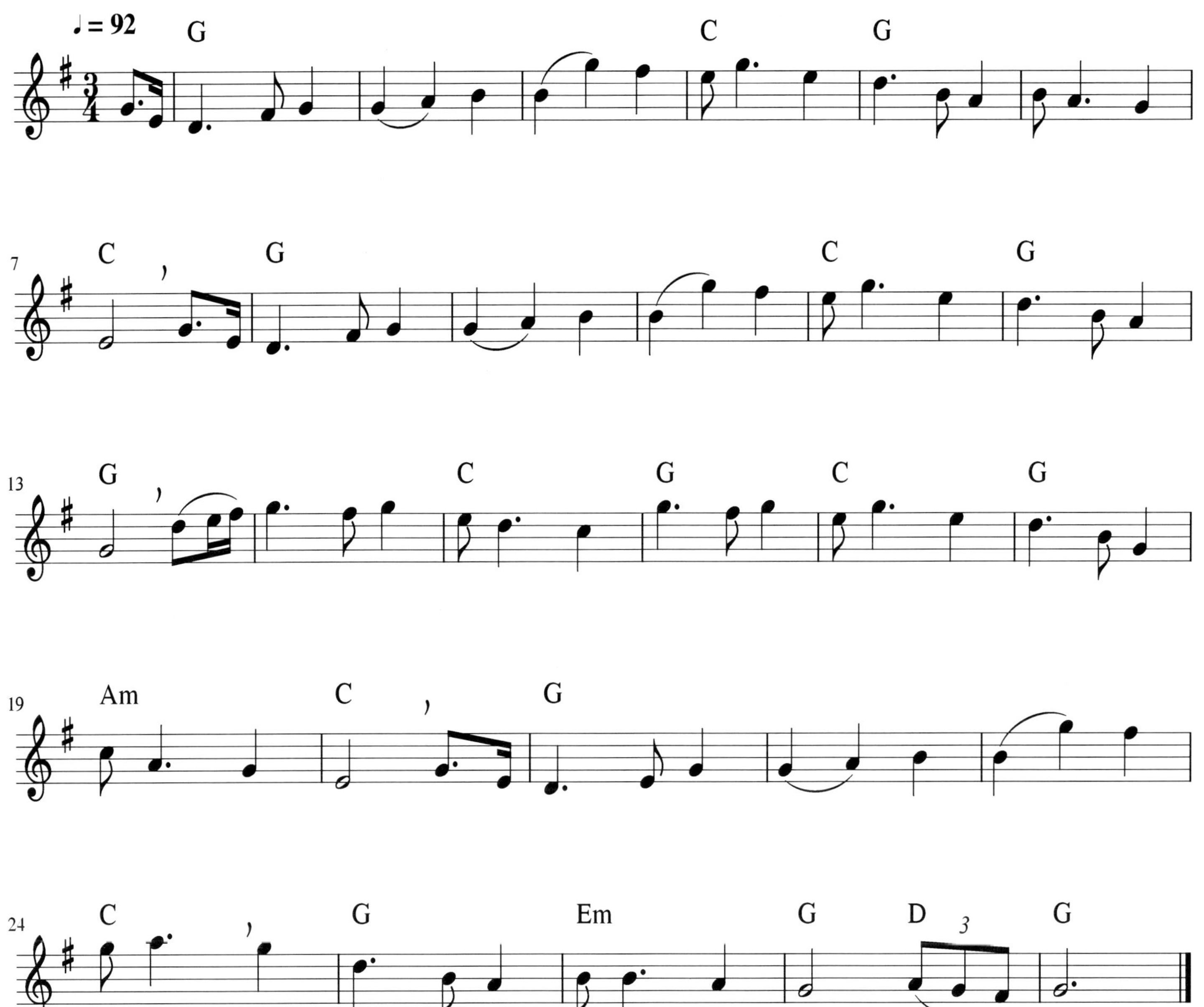

There Is a Long House at the Top of the Village

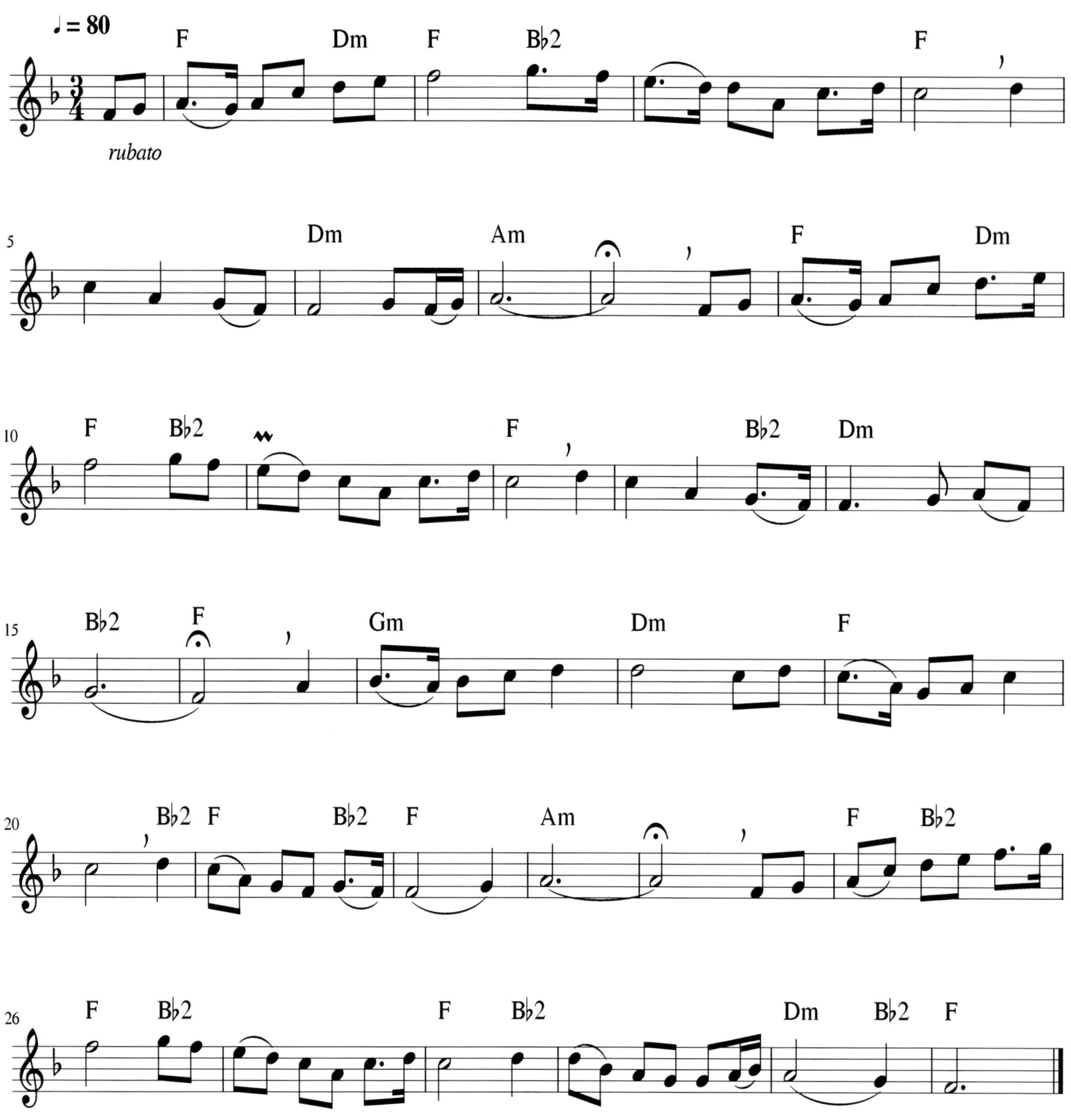

O Gentle Dove

for David

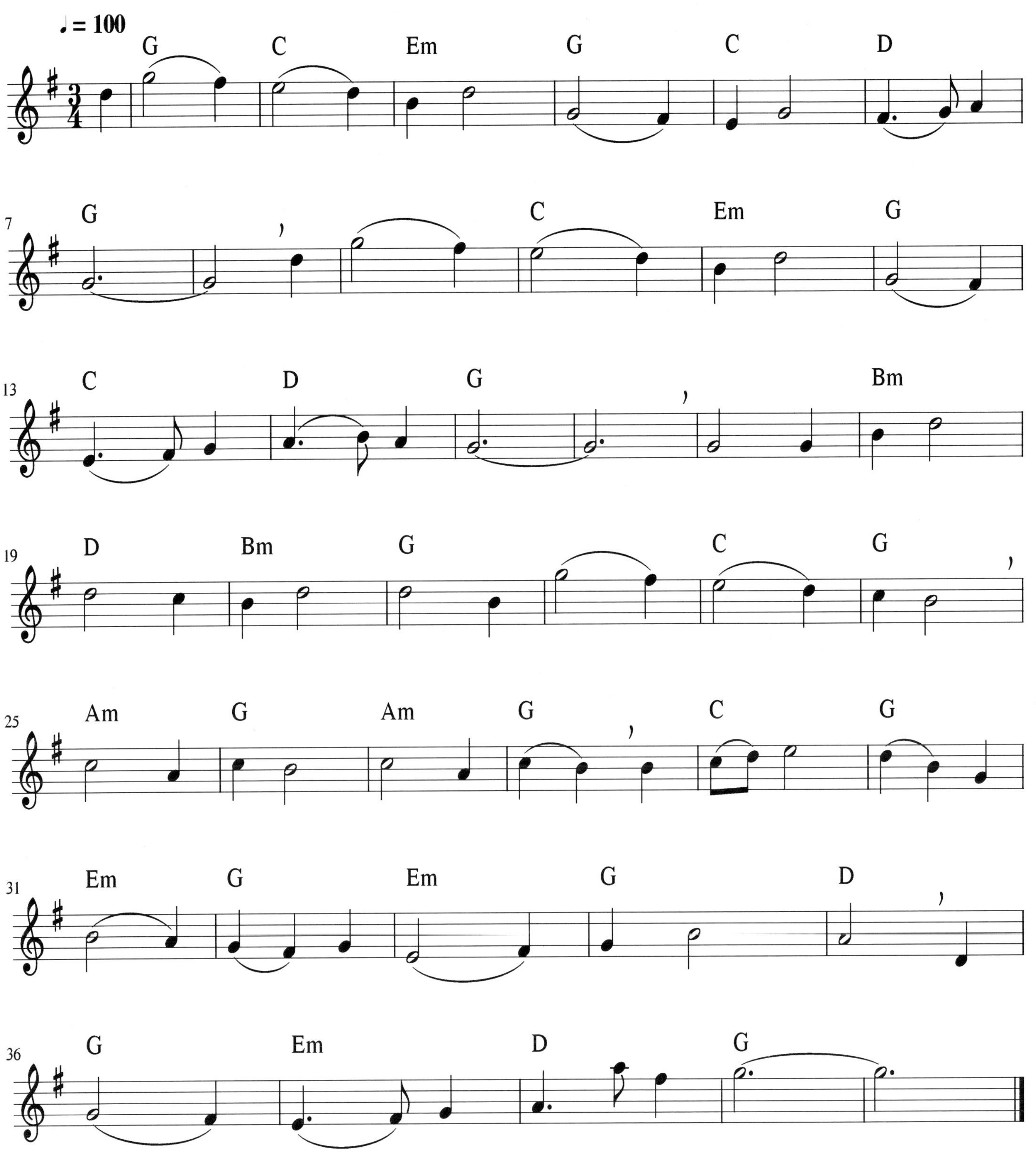

Enchanted Valley

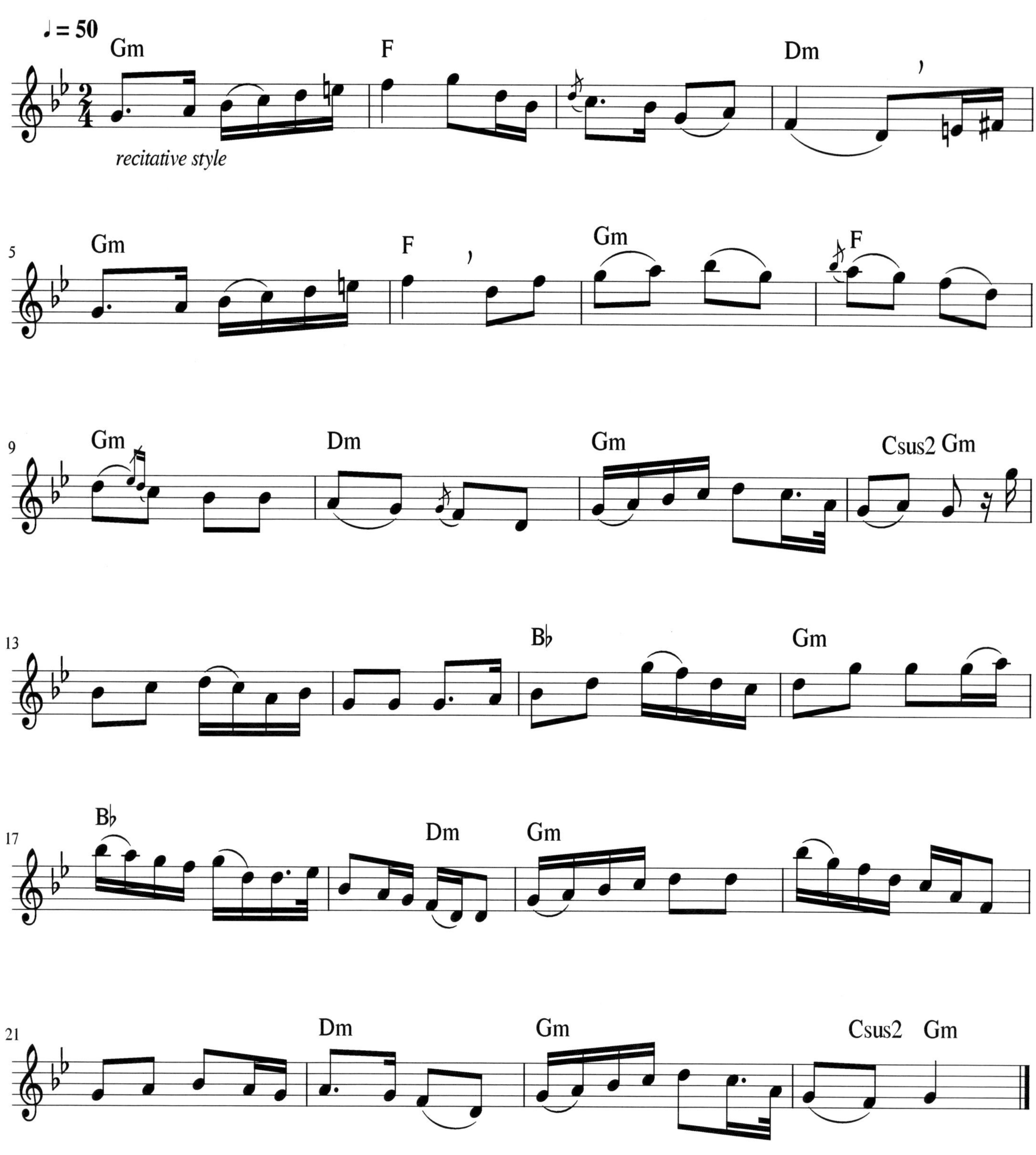

Give Me Your Hand

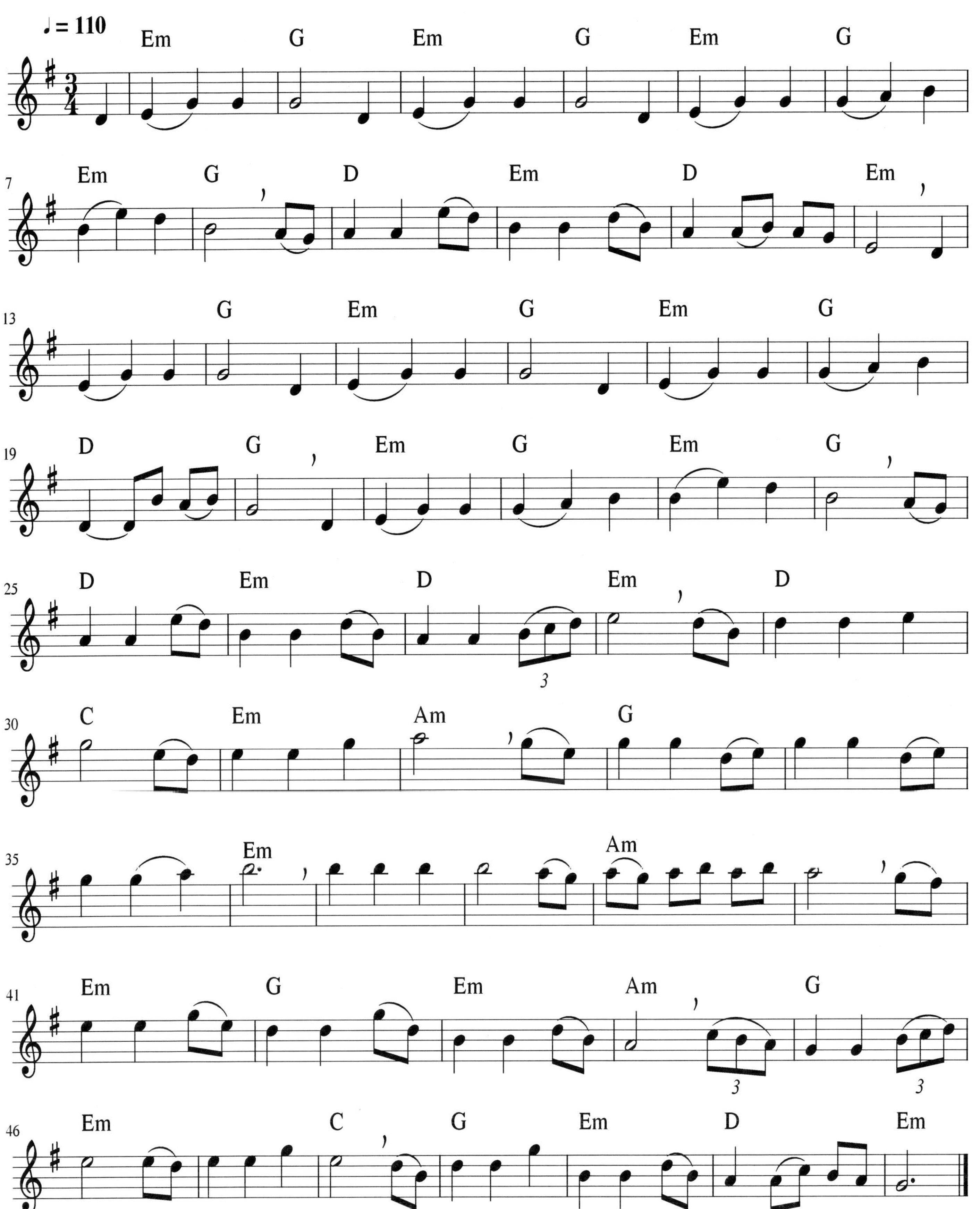

Star of the County Down

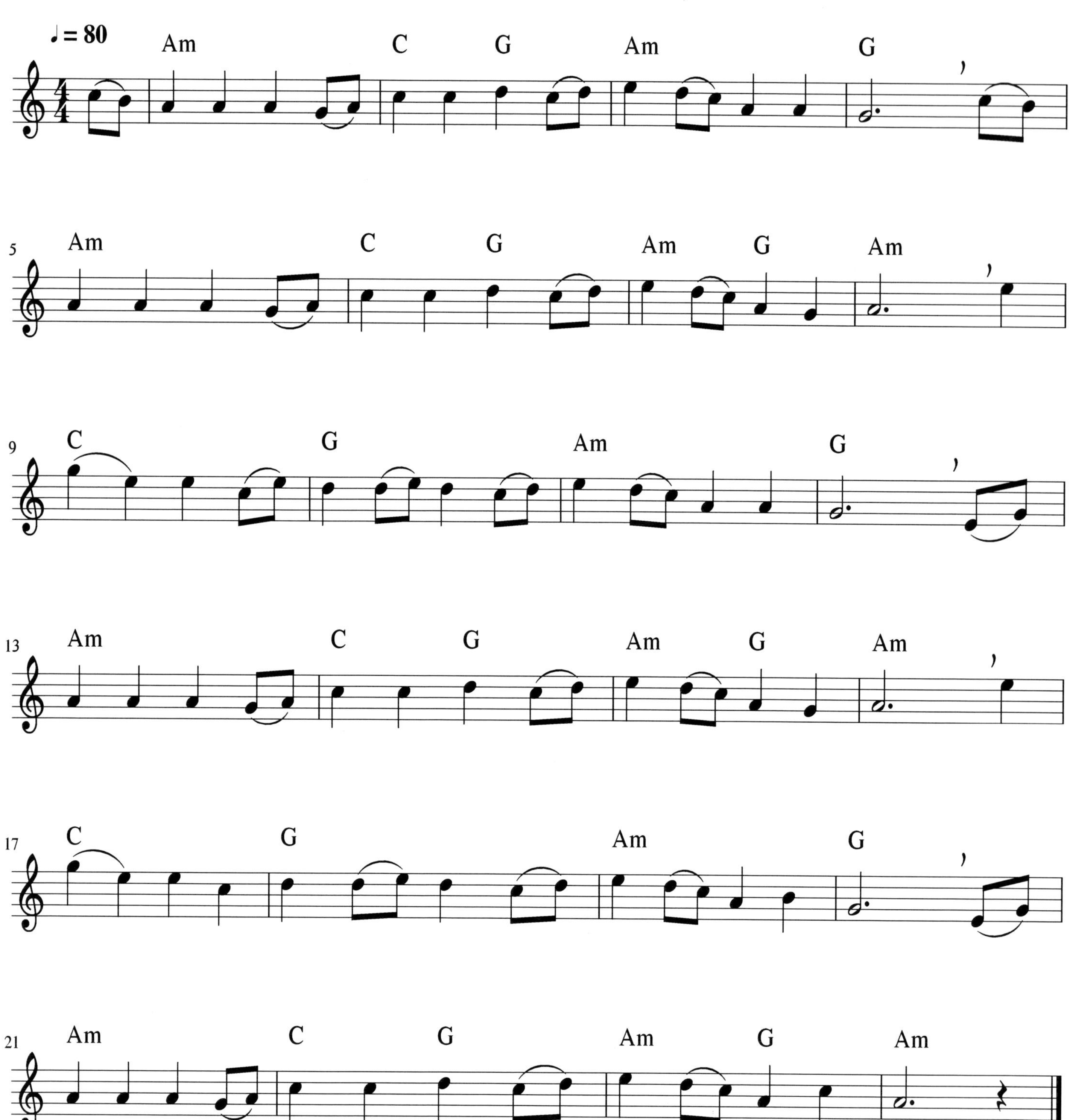

The Young Black Cow

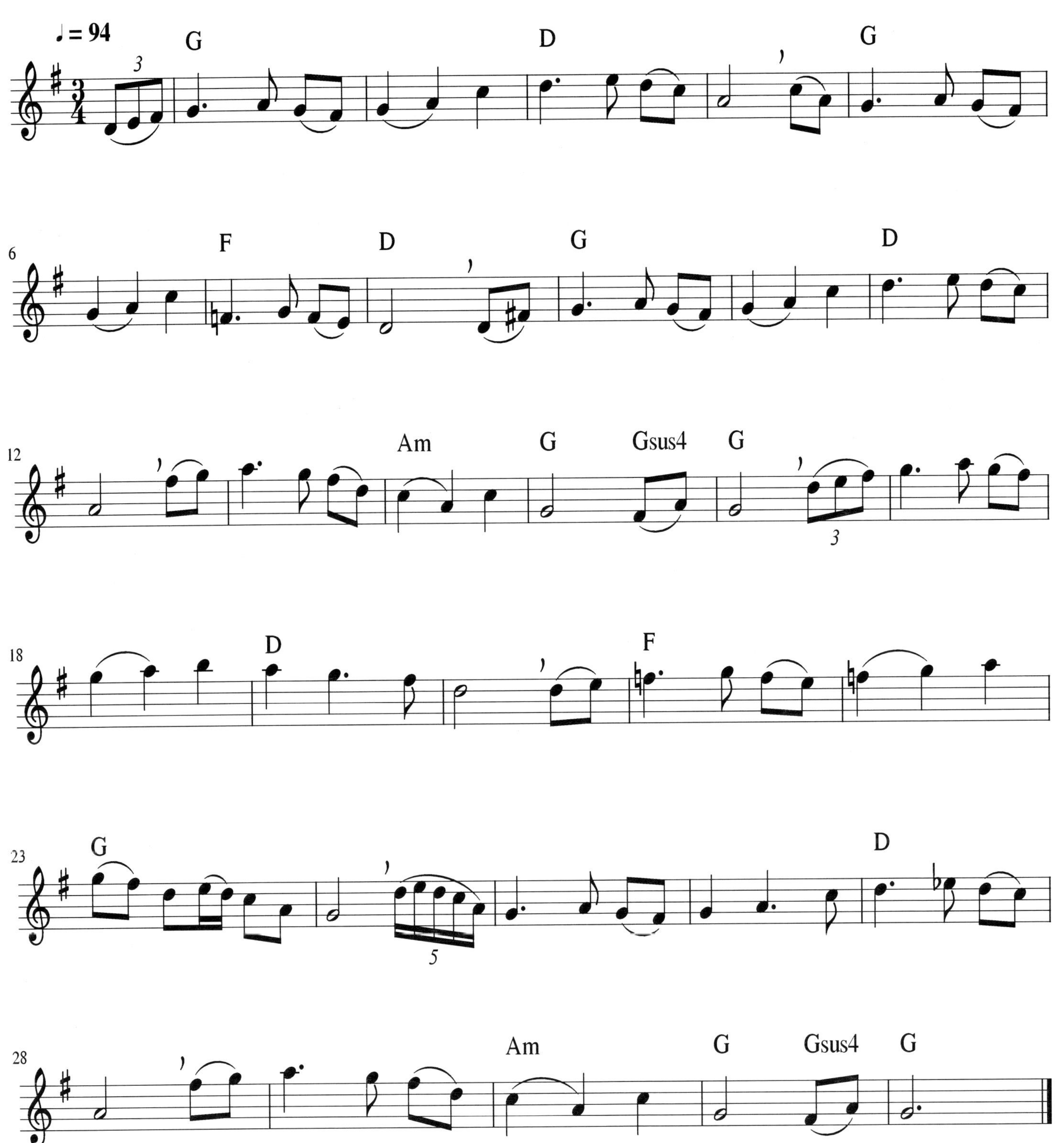

Bonny at Morn

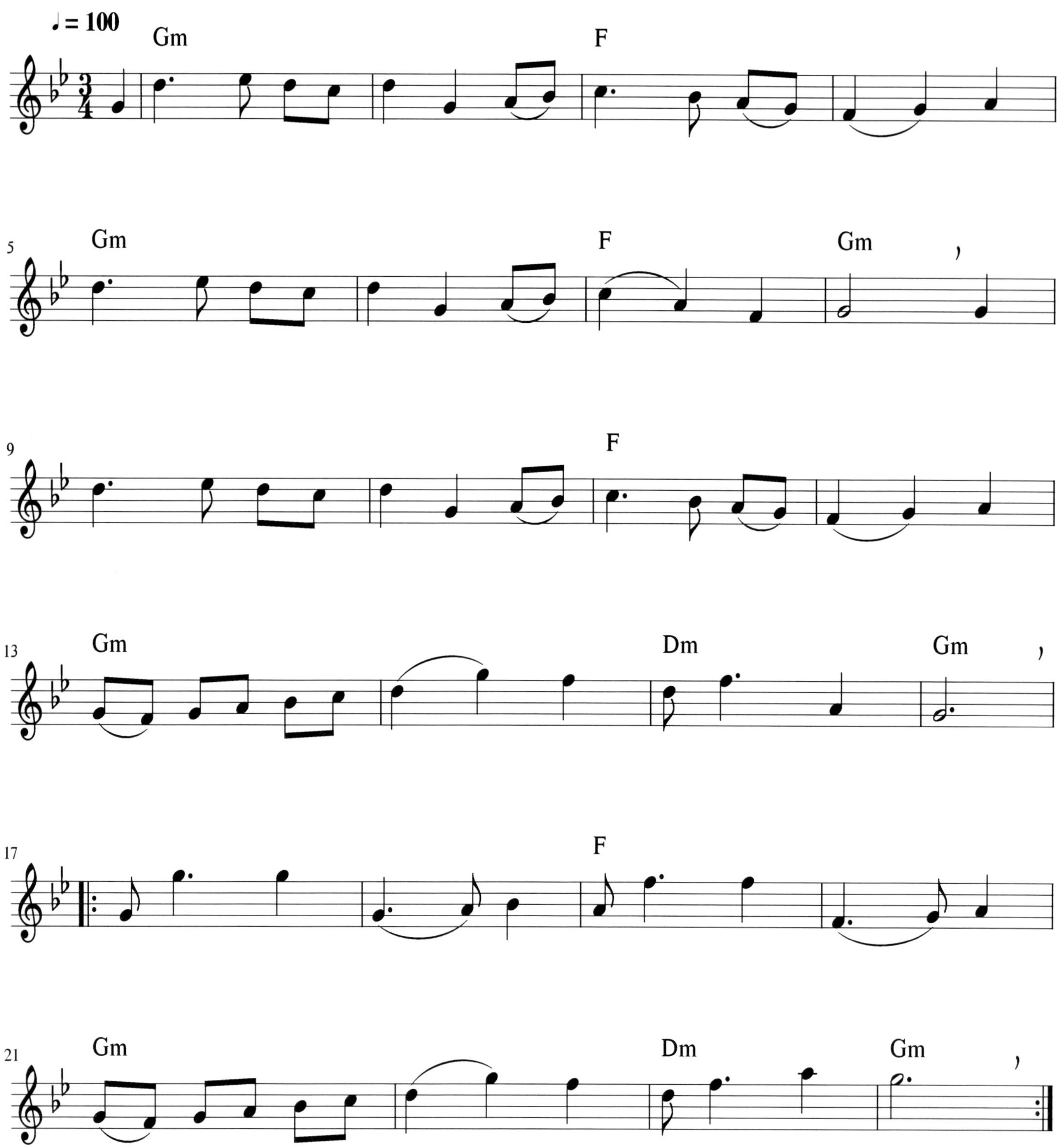

Skye Boat Song

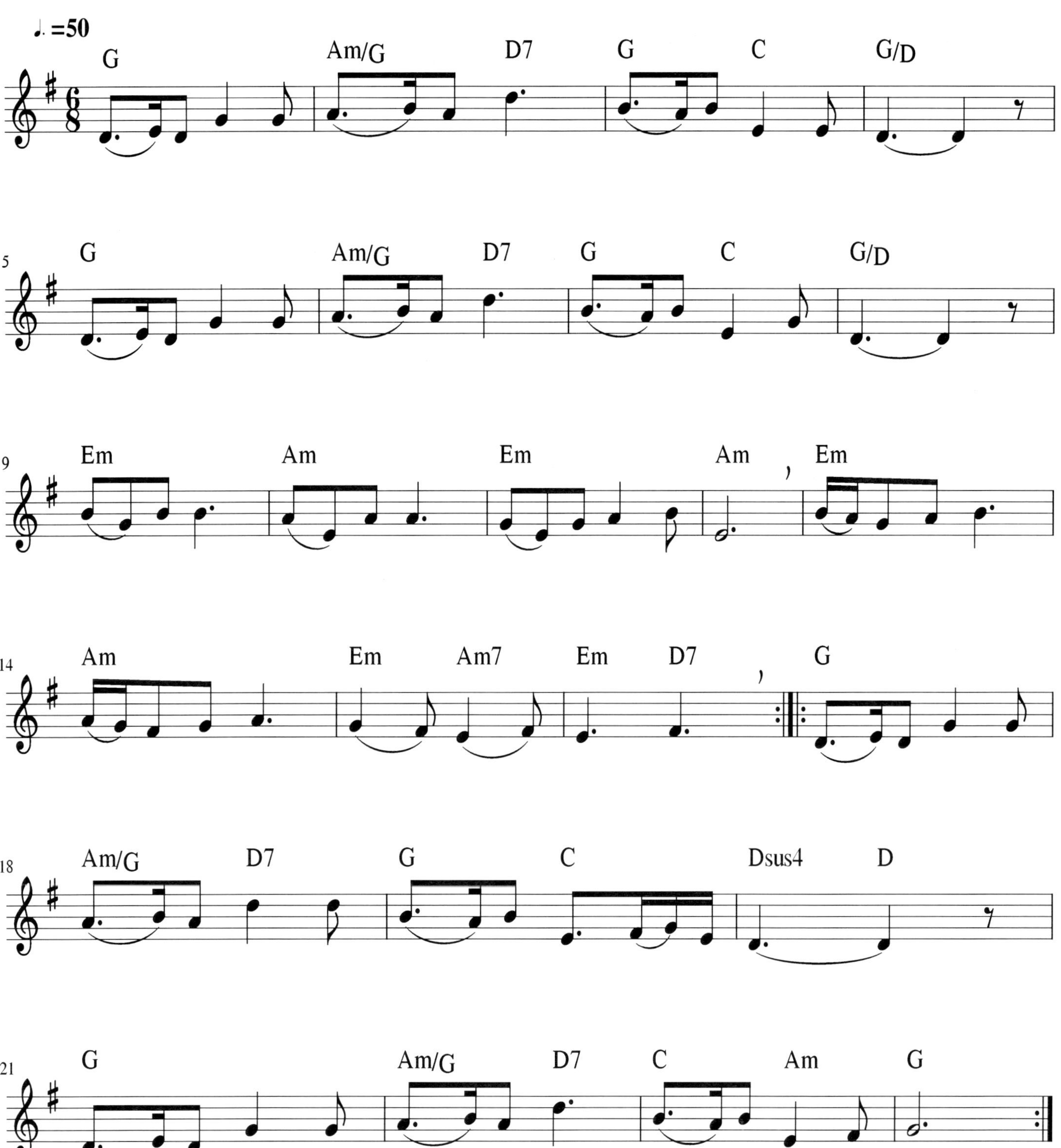

The Sheep Under the Snow

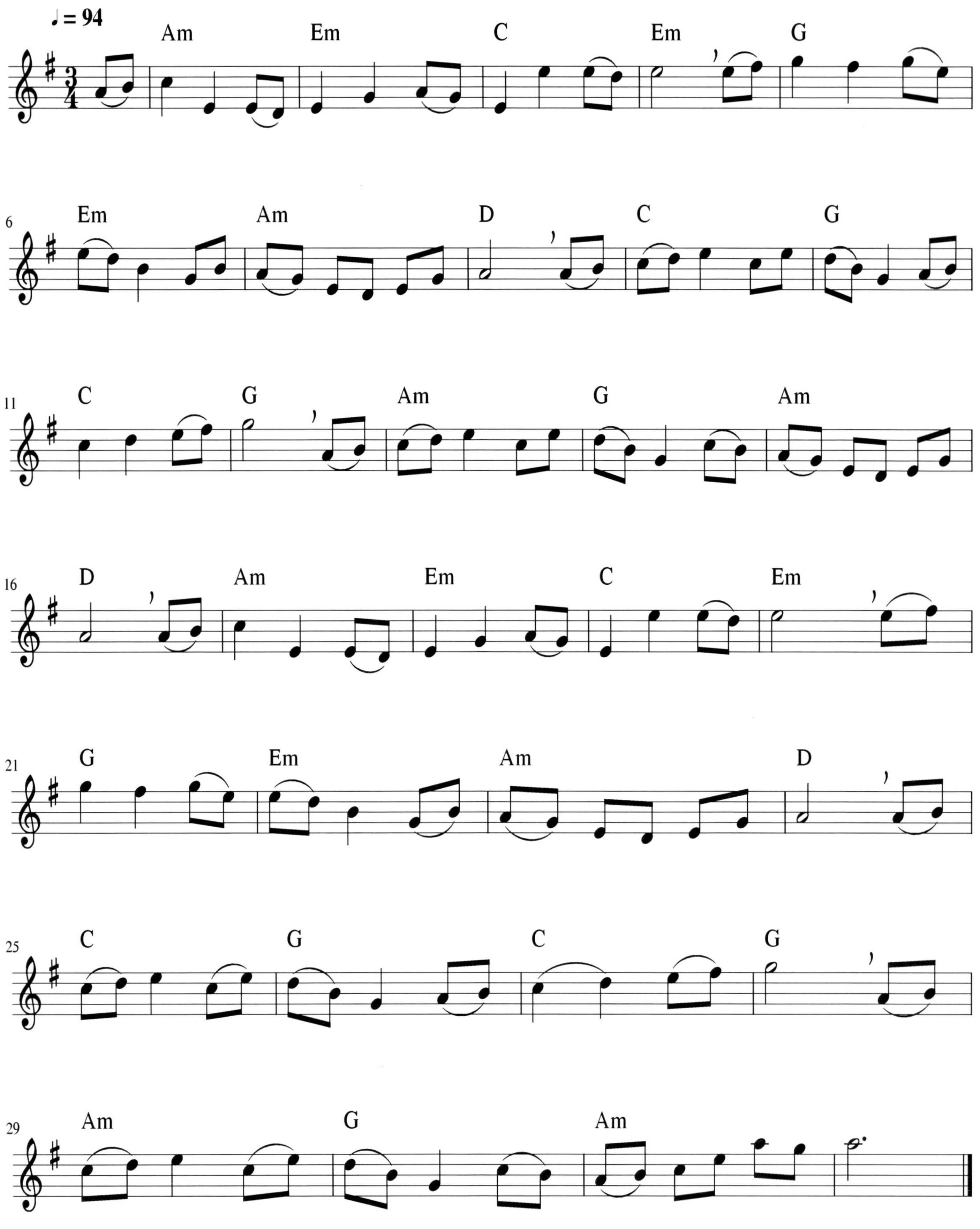

An Old Man He Courted Me

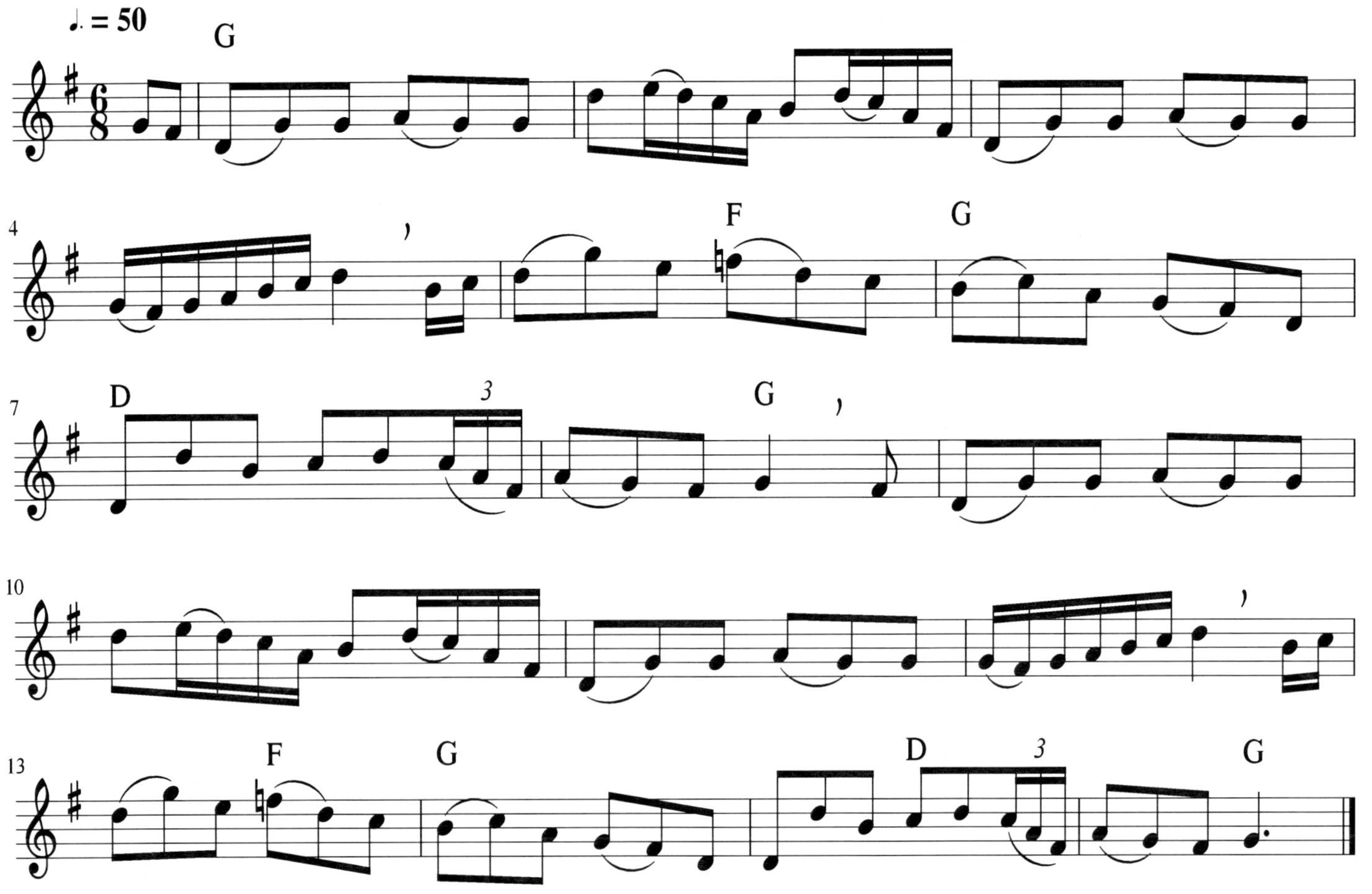

My Home

♩. = 45
B♭
E♭
F
B♭
E♭
F
B♭
E♭
F
B♭
A♭
B♭
E♭
F
B♭
E♭
F
B♭
E♭
F
B♭
A♭
B♭
Dm
E♭
B♭
E♭
B♭
Gm
B♭
A♭
B♭
Gm
B♭
A♭
B♭
ritard

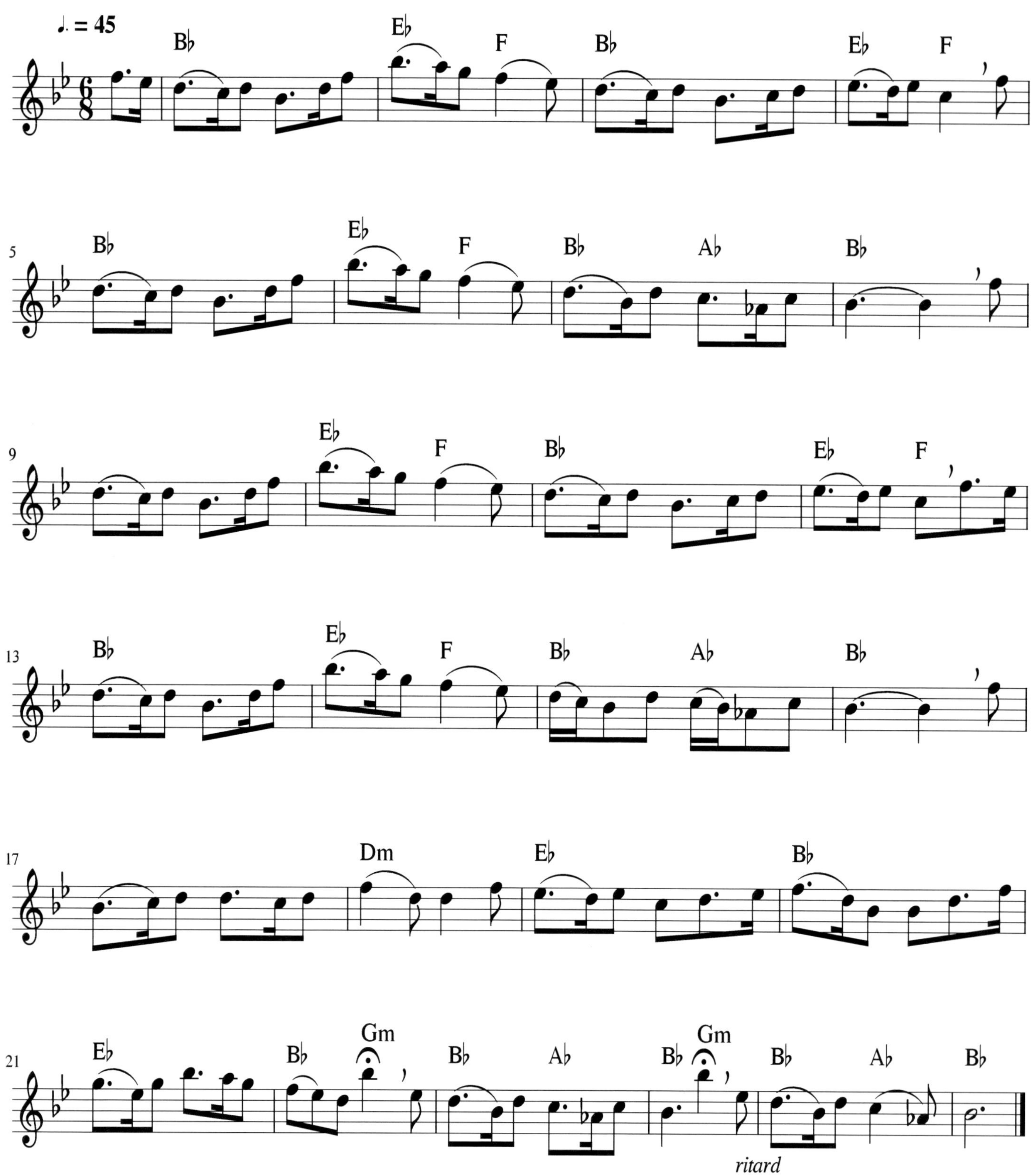

The Dawning of the Day

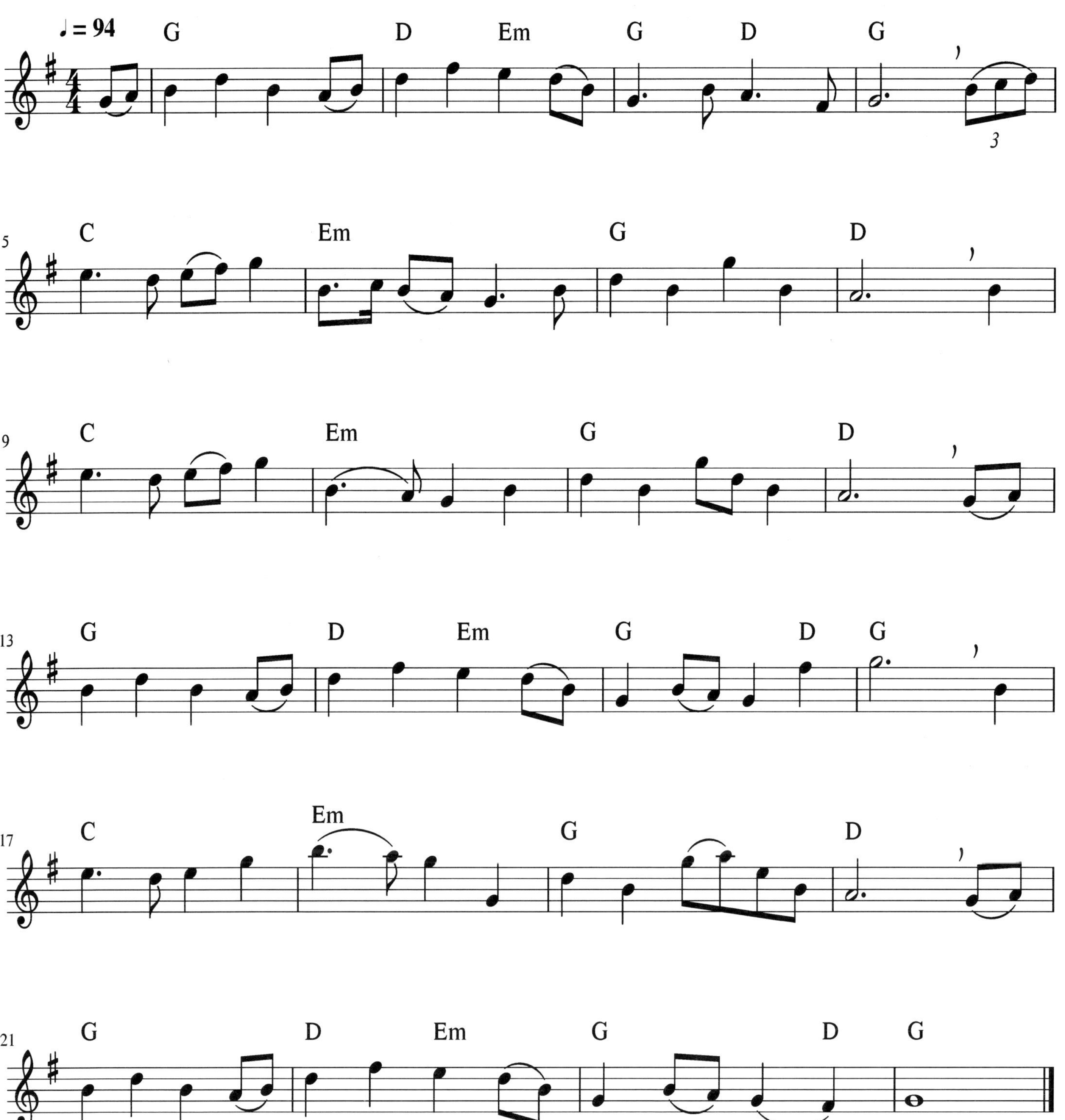

Emerald Musings

for Rhoni

Marcia Diehl

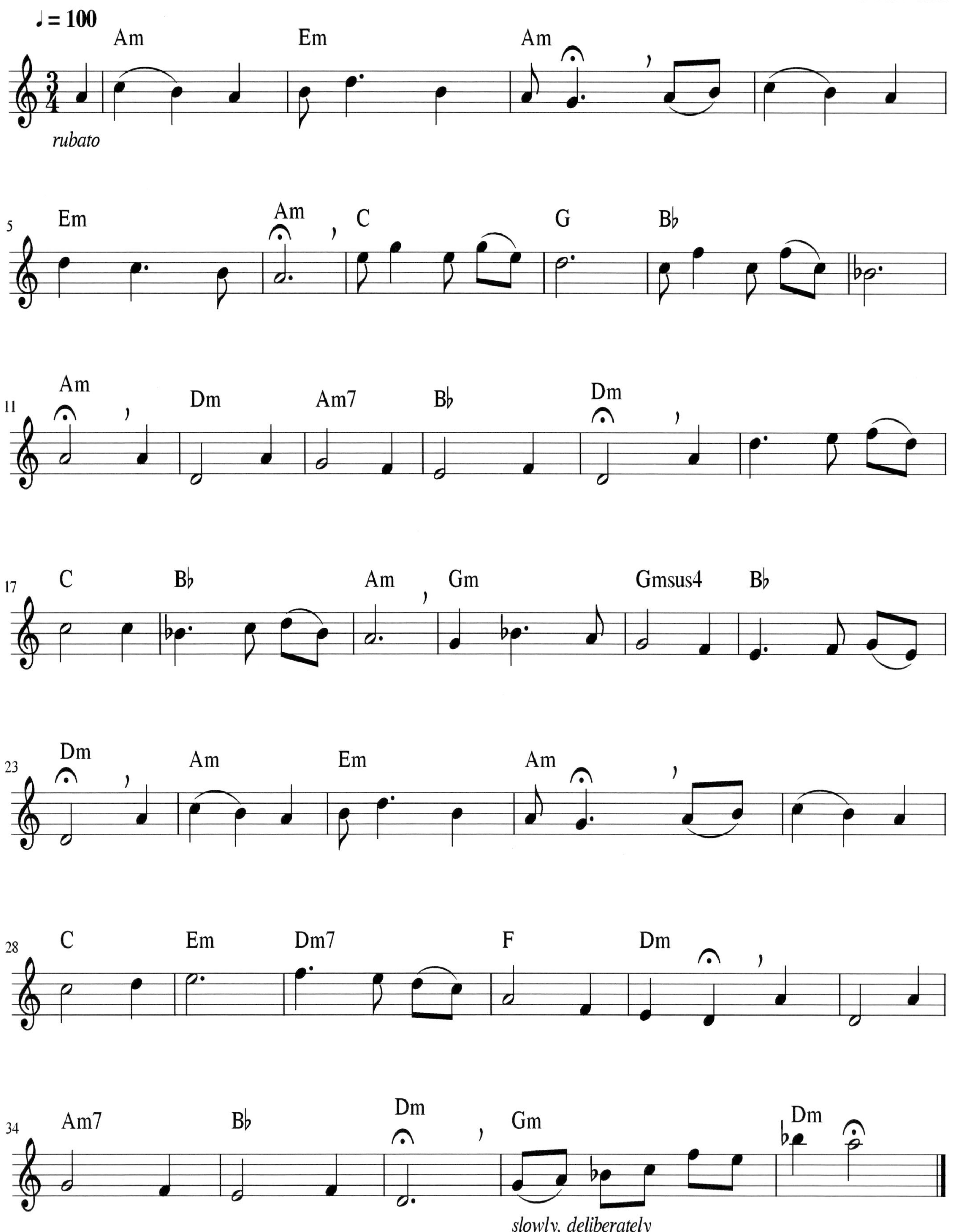